THE BLENDED FAMILY MOM

KRISTIE CARPENTER

THE BLENDED FAMILY MOM

INTERACTIVE DEVOTIONALS TO HELP YOU
'STIR AND MIX' YOUR BLENDED FAMILY

TATE PUBLISHING
AND ENTERPRISES, LLC

The Blended Family Mom
Copyright © 2013 by Kristie Carpenter. All rights reserved.

No part of this publication may be reproduced, stored in a retrieval system or transmitted in any way by any means, electronic, mechanical, photocopy, recording or otherwise without the prior permission of the author except as provided by USA copyright law.

Scripture used in this devotional is from the Zondervan NIV Study Bible, 2008 Update.

This book is designed to provide accurate and authoritative information with regard to the subject matter covered. This information is given with the understanding that neither the author nor Tate Publishing, LLC is engaged in rendering legal, professional advice. Since the details of your situation are fact dependent, you should additionally seek the services of a competent professional.

The opinions expressed by the author are not necessarily those of Tate Publishing, LLC.

Published by Tate Publishing & Enterprises, LLC
127 E. Trade Center Terrace | Mustang, Oklahoma 73064 USA
1.888.361.9473 | www.tatepublishing.com

Tate Publishing is committed to excellence in the publishing industry. The company reflects the philosophy established by the founders, based on Psalm 68:11,
"The Lord gave the word and great was the company of those who published it."

Book design copyright © 2013 by Tate Publishing, LLC. All rights reserved.
Cover design by Arjay Grecia
Interior design by Jomar Ouano

Published in the United States of America

ISBN: 978-1-62902-453-0
Family & Relationships / General
13.11.06

DEDICATION

This book is dedicated to my children—all of them. It matters not whether God gave you to me through my own flesh and blood, through marriage, or included in the precious packages of friendship—you are all so very important to me. God is using you in such a mighty way to teach, mold, shape and humble me. He is also using each of you to strengthen and embolden me to be the woman He intended. Thanks for hanging in there with me! It is my hope that I make God proud, honor my husband and then be an example to you that "all things are possible in Christ."

PREFACE

Through sacrifice comes blessing. I heard these words many years ago and have never been able to shake them out of my head. As I look at life, though, I have found that everything in life that is worthwhile requires sacrifice. Your blended family requires sacrifice. Through your sacrifice and perseverance, God will bless you and your family.

I am praying that you will join me in filling ourselves with God's Word and knowing that you are not alone! Our stories are all different and yet we share this common bond of emotion and struggle that comes from two broken families being melded into one. I am hoping that you will find honesty of thought in this devotional book along with humor—albeit borderline slanderous or scandalous! Finally, I am praying that you find encouragement to go through your day and keep up the good fight. I am right there alongside you—still fighting to the end when either Jesus returns or the kids all move out!

INTRODUCTION

This was written in a format that will hopefully be helpful in propelling you forward in this very important life task of "mom". I have broken it down into baby steps. Every week is split up into five days.

Day 1's are the devotional part of the week, including Scripture, a short story, and then a written prayer to guide you in your prayer time.

Day 2's are the Scripture memory days. Write them on note cards and place on your bathroom mirrors, refrigerators, or wherever. Encourage the kids to learn these with you.

Day 3's are usually planning and preparing days for an upcoming activity with your family.

Day 4's are to implement the activity you planned and prepared for.

Day 5's are to take a minute to sit and jot down your thoughts about the week and the outcome of the week's activity. Also take the opportunity to write down some praises and prayer requests.

Day by day, week by week, it is my prayer that you will start forming such a strong bond with this new family unit. Remember, you are not alone. Your outrageous thoughts and feelings have been thought and felt before. The desire to give up and walk out is not uncommon. This book is to get you through these times…because what lies ahead can be truly beautiful!

WEEK 1

Day 1

He chose us in Him before the creation of the world.

Ephesians 1:4a

I was adopted and live with the reality that my birth parents were not married and either didn't want me or couldn't keep me. So God hand picked my adopted parents to come and save me. God placed me into their loving arms, and I had all the love and care a child could ever need or want. He knew they would raise me up in church, teach me about strength, endurance, morals, and the value of commitment. Some of these characteristics "stuck" more than others, but on the whole I believe I've done okay!

Roles have now reversed. My mom has Alzheimer's disease and is steadily getting worse. I am so very thankful that God opened doors for me and my children to move to their town—to be with them in their later years- to help out.

It is strange not to be able to lean on them as I always have. I'm the strong one now in the relationship—providing Mom with avenues to entertain her and giving Dad a much needed break periodically.

After a particularly draining day with Mom, I was thanking God for picking them to be my parents—for loving me so much that He placed me with such wonderful, loving, caring people. It was right then that my heart was filled with these words.

> I picked you. I knew you would be there for your parents when they needed you the most. I knew you would make the sacrifices needed to move to where they lived, love them and care for them.

I remember feeling so honored and humbled that God would pick me to minister to these two people—people that He cares about greatly and loves perfectly and completely. His plan for them included me.

God has picked you. We are all in positions within someone else's life to be that instrument that God uses to love them. Because He has picked you—you are in a position of honor—serving God and then being entrusted to serve His precious children. Your blended family is no exception. He picked you because He knew this family needed you!

Lord, I am thankful for those that you have picked to be my family. Help me to realize, though, that You have picked me. I have a very important task ahead of me—which is to love this family and serve them and do my part to keep us together and strong. You picked me for this task because You knew I could do it. Thank You, Father. Please give me what I need today for my mission.

Day 2

Memorize Ephesians 1:4a today. Make it personal by saying "me" where the "us" is.

Day 3

Write your family's names on sticky notes or post cards and then tape them in places in your home or at work, where you will see them periodically. Every time you see one, stop and thank God that they are in your life and thank God that He picked you to be in theirs.

Day 4 Through Sacrifice comes Blessing

Do something today or plan to do something over the weekend that requires you to serve your family—something extra. You could bake cookies, plan a picnic, paint a wall in a child's bedroom, etc. When we make the time (and take the time) to go the extra mile, it comes back tenfold!

Day 5 Your Thoughts and Prayers

_____

_____

_____

_____

_____

_____

WEEK 2

Day 1

Praise be to the God and Father of our Lord Jesus Christ, the Father of compassion and the God of all comfort, who comforts us in all our troubles, so that we can comfort those in any trouble with the comfort we ourselves have received from God.

II Corinthians 1:3-5

I am writing this devotional book because of these verses. I have been through the death of a husband, finding out my two children have kidney disease, being a single mom, and being in a marriage as a wife and step mom in a blended family. Through it all, God has been there. Through it all God has guided me and tenderly cared for me. Through it all God has called me to share my experiences and His grace in all things—to you. I call this "living out loud"—opening up my life to you—even the good, bad, and the ugly.

My first husband died at the young age of 32. I was numb and yet had so many emotions swirling around in my head and heart. I remember many nights sitting alone in my living room and just crying out to God: "I don't like you right now… I don't understand… how could this be your perfect will? What about those two precious children who now have no father?" Through these raw emotions, though, I remained constantly fixed on the fact that my God is in control. He has me. He won't forget me or forsake me. So day by day I would cling to that. Now the kids and I have a compassion for those who have lost spouses/parents.

You may be at a rough place today. A blended family just seems to multiply the problems and challenges that face us. I urge you to lift your eyes to the heavens and cry out to God, "Thank You. Thank You for knowing where I am; for Your control in this situation; for Your power to do a good work through all of this." God will certainly carry you through the rough times. Then you need to "live out loud" and share your story with other women in your same position, who are going through similar situations.

> Lord, You are an amazing God. Your plan is perfect for my life and I want to acknowledge that You are in control. I don't understand this place in my life, but know that You will carry me through and then give me the strength and courage to share with others what You have done in my life.

Day 2

Memorize II Corinthians 1:3-5. Remember, we go through situations and experiences and then we are to share with and comfort others. In other words, "live out loud".

Day 3

Make a list of people you know—or know of—who have been hurt by death or divorce and then share it with your family and ask them to pray for these people. Talk about how God can do a good work in their lives just as He has done in yours. Romans 8:28 is true, "And we know that in all things God works for the good of those who love Him, who have been called according to His purpose."

Day 4 Through Sacrifice comes Blessing

From yesterday's list, pick one person or family from it and then have your family do a random act of kindness for them this weekend. Your family may want to prepare a meal for them; the kids may want to pick some fresh flowers and put in a vase; or offer to do yard work, wash their car, or some other project. Working together provides avenues for conversation and family bonding.

Day 5 Your Thoughts and Prayers

WEEK 3

Day 1

But Noah found favor in the eyes of the Lord.

Genesis 6:8

Can you just picture this nice little community, rolling sand dunes, friendly neighbors and a dry heat? Real dry—boating was not a recreational activity back in Noah's day but we see him sawing and hammering away. Of course we start gossiping that we always thought he was a bit "off". Noah, his wife and kids surely heard the whispers and the laughter aimed at them. I imagine that even going grocery hunting had become a depressing struggle for Mrs. Noah. But this family stayed together, stayed strong, endured the teasing and name calling, and continued to help Noah put together the boat God had told him to build. Sacrifice.

You and your family may not be building a boat, but you are building a family and a strong home/safe haven for all involved. You have God's 'blueprints' available for this task—His Word. Keep listening to God. So many times we start listening to what the world says we should do and frankly, I believe that is where most of the problems begin. Noah may have even thought himself loony, but that didn't matter to him. At the end of the day, he knew that whatever he thought, whatever other people thought or said; he was still doing what God had called him to do. Oh by the way, this did take Noah a llllooonnnggg time! Now picture the magnificent boat that Noah and his family have completed, along with a menagerie of animals, and it starts sprinkling. Noah may have looked out among the many neighbors that had teased him and ostracized his family and thought… "how long can you tread water?"

End result? Blessing. Noah's family was saved. They started the earth's population all over! Plus, his story in the Bible is told over and over from generation to generation.

Blessing. Keep building. Don't stray from the plans God has given you. There will be people who will tell you to give up and get out. Don't listen to them. Every night I want you to go to bed knowing that no matter what you think, or what others think or say, you are doing what God has called you to do … to be this family's mom. Keep building, cuz I smell rain!

> Lord, some days the sacrifice seems so hard. Help me today to remember that from sacrifice comes blessing. I am where you have placed me … bless me this day, please.

Day 2

Memorize Genesis 6:8. We can also find favor in the eyes of the Lord when we walk in obedience—just as Noah did.

Day 3

Building anything usually takes a plan. Sit down with your husband and begin the 'blueprints' to building your strong family. For example, Dan and I have family 'blueprints' that include family night every Sunday evening; we don't allow R-rated movies to be watched in our home; we participate in our local church every Sunday; curfews are established and followed or consequences take place. These are just a few of ours—make your own!

Day 4 Through Sacrifice comes Blessing

You and your husband share your family 'blueprints' with your children. When everyone knows the plans, it is easier to move towards the goal!

Day 5 Your Thoughts and Prayers

_____
_____
_____
_____
_____
_____

WEEK 4

Day 1

Let us not love with words or tongue but with actions and in truth.

I John 3:18

Love is an action. Love is baking cookies.

My blended family is a little different than most; my step daughter is twenty-four and has three children and lives in a guest house that God provided for us when my husband and I first got married; my step son is twenty and has Asperger's Syndrome and is on a 10-year probation for making a mistake. Loving these kids has been challenging for me at times. I have prayed that God would just make me loving towards them, but I didn't seem to get a clear response from Him. Then I remembered that love is not an emotion that just shows up. We have to take steps to get there. So I baked cookies.

My step son loves treats. I once left Oreo's in the shape of a smiley face on a paper plate with a thank you note for him and he came and gave me the biggest bear hug ever! I then decided that even though he has an emotional/mental disorder, I could still connect with him and show him love through actions that he relates to. Baking cookies together was a good start!

How can you actively love your step kids today? Believe me, you may not 'feel the love' but when we just spur ahead and take 'baby steps' towards our step children, we find a joy that is only God-given. I find a sudden smile on my lips and a feeling in my heart that God is saying to me, "Good job my child… I believe you are starting to get it!"

> Lord, help me to actively love my family. Fill my head with ideas that will not only show love to all my family, but help me to 'feel' the love also.

Day 2

Memorize I John 3:18. Get ready to act!

Day 3

All children are different. Find out what each one of yours likes to do or likes to eat and then plan to do that activity or fix that food for each one. Look at the rest of your week and then set aside time to do the activity for each child individually. This will be easy unless you have 14 kids!

Day 4 Through Sacrifice comes Blessing

Start actively loving your kids with your plans from yesterday.

Day 5 Your Thoughts and Prayers

_____
_____
_____
_____
_____
_____

WEEK 5

Day 1

> Then they (the older women) can train the younger women to love their husbands and children, to be self-controlled and pure, to be busy at home, to be kind, and to be subject to their husbands, so that no one will malign the word of God.
>
> Titus 2: 4-5

These verses have taken on a new meaning to me since I have become a step mom. Not only do I want my own children to see me try to do things God's way, but the same goes for my step children. I have seen my step daughter grow in leaps and bounds just by being there for her, listening to her and trying to give her godly advice. I love the fact that God wired us women to love, nurture, encourage, and mentor those who come along behind us. We are such Mother Hens!

Our children are watching how we seek God, run our homes, conduct business, and build relationships. Our impact on them is tremendous. Knowing this, I pray that you will always choose to take time to mentor—listen even when there are so many things that still need to be done; hug when you need a hug yourself; guide and give godly advice even when you are dog tired. Remember, there will always be more 'stuff' to do, but our kids are only under our 'wings' for a short time. So, Mother Hen, go tend to your 'chicks'!

> Lord, help me today to be a godly woman who places the needs of my family over my desire to get the laundry caught up and the floors cleaned. I am your instrument to love, nurture, and teach these children. Help me to take advantage of every opportunity with them.

Day 2

Memorize Titus 2:4-5. You may not have an education degree, but you are definitely a teacher to those around you.

Day 3

If your children are old enough, plan to get them all involved in learning how to bake something or build something. My son and I decided to make a kitty condo just from the scrap material we already had around the house. It turned out to be a carpeted three-story masterpiece. The time spent with him was priceless.

Day 4 Through Sacrifice comes Blessing

Take your plans from yesterday and get going!

Day 5 Your Thoughts and Prayers

_____
_____
_____
_____
_____
_____

WEEK 6

DAY 1

...she provides food for her family; she considers a field and buys it; she sets about her work vigorously; she speaks with wisdom and faithful instruction is on her tongue; she watches over the affairs of her household; a woman who fears the Lord is to be praised.

Proverbs 31: 15-31 (randomly)

Yes, basically these verses sum up my existence—cooking, cleaning, buying groceries and then raising our children up with all the proper lectures at the proper times. I love the last line—"a woman who fears the Lord is to be praised." I think that King Lemuel's mother included that to remind him that if he ever found the perfect Proverbs 31 woman that does all the stuff we do—she better be praised!

Seriously, you are the 'matriarch' of your home which includes taking care of your husband, his/yours/ya'lls kids, and your home. You also need to take care of yourself—set boundaries. This was so tough for me to do but was desperately needed. Within our new family unit, there needed to be a place where children were restricted; a place where I didn't have to pick up a child's dirty sock or a left behind toy; a place of relaxation and calm—romance. Please make your bedroom a place where you and your husband can 'get away from it all'. Remove the clutter and chaos and replace it with soft lighting, candles, and pleasing aromas. We also removed our desk with our computer on it so that we would not be drawn to sit on the computer for extended periods of time checking that last e-mail or playing one more game of solitaire! (that would be my vice!) This 'sanctuary' has helped me to find my sanity time and time again and my husband looks forward to his "down time" within the comfort of our room. There are enough common areas in our house to talk, play, help, encourage and love on our kids. Make sure your bedroom becomes a place of refuge from the world for you and your husband—a place for romance to blossom and quiet conversations of hopes and dreams to be shared.

> Lord, You have shown us love by setting boundaries for us—for our good, for our protection, and for our growth. I pray that You would help me to set a boundary that my husband's and my bedroom is off limits to the kids. Help me to make this room a haven from work, the ugliness of the world and the problems that we are facing right now.

Day 2

Read Proverbs 31. We are to be productive and use the gifts and talents that God has given us. We should strive to be smart and savvy. But I believe that we should never lose sight of verse 30—we can do all sorts of things... but when we live our lives in reverence and awe of our Lord, then we are to be praised.

Day 3

Take a good look at you and your husband's bedroom. Is it a place of rest and tranquility? Is it free of clutter and chaos? If it is lacking in these areas, make a plan to transform this space into something special for you and your man! This may require moving furniture and computers. It may require getting rid of a million knick-knacks on your dresser. And I know you wouldn't have to do this... but it may require finding a place for the dirty clothes other than the floor or chair or the dusty treadmill. (Get the treadmill out of there too!) Your goal is romance and calm.

Day 4 Through Sacrifice comes Blessing

You planned yesterday for a new and improved bedroom. Take today and the weekend to make it happen. Even if you only clear clutter, it is a step in the right direction!

DAY 5 YOUR THOUGHTS AND PRAYERS

_____
_____
_____
_____
_____
_____

WEEK 7

DAY 1

> Remember this: Whoever sows sparingly will also reap sparingly, and whoever sows generously will also reap generously.
>
> 2 Corinthians 9:6

Anything worth while takes time—and sometimes a lot of blood, sweat and tears too. A blended family is no different. You can give a little or you can give a lot. It depends on what kind of "harvest" you want.

When Dan and I started dating, my son got excited about the possibility of having a dad again. I guess when you're the only guy living with a couple of drama queen girls, that prospect looks really inviting! Eight months later, Dan and I married and joined our "forces" into a battalion. Yes, that word means a military group ready for battle—except our battle was one within the ranks.

As accepting as my son was to this new group, my daughter was on the opposite end of the spectrum. She had grown accustomed to our little threesome as well as not having to answer to anyone else but me. She definitely was not ready to open up her heart to another family coming in and taking over her space and place. As you can imagine, this brought about one of the first hurdles in our marriage.

Dan kept trying to be nice and encouraging; including her in conversations and family outings, but she made it known that she didn't want to do any blending into this new family.

I remember a particular evening when it was time to say our goodnights to the kids. Dan wasn't sure if he wanted to tell my daughter goodnight. He told me that he was tired of "going half way" when she wasn't willing to go the other half. I told him that since we were the adults, it was our job to go however far we needed to in order to reach our kids—and sometimes that means stretching all the way—"sowing generously". Dan began to take extra steps towards her—giving her a hug when she was aloof; just hanging out to engage her in conversation and show his interest in her life; asking her advice and opinions—and truly listening to her.

Well, Dan stretched and sowed and my daughter responded. It has taken a couple of years, but now they share phone conversations, text messaging, and more importantly, hugs and "I love you's". My daughter respects the husband he is to me and is so appreciative that he took the time and had the patience to reach her heart. Love was sown generously and the harvest is a beautiful relationship!

As parents, we see the world in black and white. Our kids, when placed into a blended family, see a lot of gray. It is our job to sow generously into their lives to help them see the love and security of their new family. And remember, once you have sown a seed, it doesn't stop there; watering, fertilizing, pruning... and then the harvest!

> Lord, please help me to sow generously into our children's lives. Give me the power to stretch out to reach them, no matter how far that looks.

Day 2

Memorize II Corinthians 9:6. Get ready to "sow"!

Day 3

Hopefully your family is all "mixing" well together. If there are some "oil and vinegar" relationships, discuss with your husband how you or he can stretch out further to envelope this child that is having a hard time wanting to be in the mix. Discuss this with hubby today and formulate some good ideas and plans for "Operation Blend"!

Day 4 Through Sacrifice comes Blessing

As you probably already suspect, I am going to ask you to start your "Operation Blend" project today. Like Dan, it may just mean allowing ten minutes in the evening to ask about your child's day or activities involved in. Another good idea is to find this child's "love language" and help the new parent love him in this way. The book, The Five Love Languages, by Gary Chapman, is an absolutely wonderful way to find your child's love language as well as your husbands and even your own!

DAY 5 YOUR THOUGHTS AND PRAYERS

_____

_____

_____

_____

_____

_____

WEEK 8

Day 1

His master replied, 'Well done, good and faithful servant! You have been faithful with a few things; I will put you in charge of many things. Come and share your master's happiness!"

Matthew 25:21

How many of us can "bring home the bacon, fry it up in a pan, and never let him forget he's a man"? The woman personified in this well-known song was obviously not a mom in a blended family!

I'm just gonna throw this out at you... You need time. Your new family will bring about so many different feelings, experiences, trials, and joys. You need to be able to take this all in... focus on each child to see where they are at and what they might be needing; focus on your husband to make sure your marriage is priority and you are both living that in front of the children; focus on making sure you get the rest, exercise, and, yes, pampering you need to be able to juggle all the new facets of your family. I'm not suggesting that you give up your job and all other extracurricular activities in your life, but I want you to consider the impact of today's verse on your life in relation to your family. I truly believe that when we work first and hardest on the home front, all other things will fall into place. When you have a war zone at home, it can be rather difficult to focus at work. In I Timothy 3:12, it says, "a deacon must be the husband of but one wife and must manage his children and his household well." In other words, before a man could be a deacon in his church, he had to show that he could take care of the basics—his own family and home. What if we all lived like that today?

I thought I was one tough cookie before I remarried and started this blended family thing. Oh, how I laugh at my naivety now! It has taken lots of love, prayer and even counseling to get me through these years. I do believe, though, that most of the successes that we have encountered have been because we scaled our lives back and just tried to focus on being there for each other.

God wants us to be a family—a strong, loving, caring, growing, compassionate family. I also want to hear Him say, "Well done my good and faithful servant."

> Lord, please give me the wisdom to know where and how to scale back my life so that I may focus on this family. Show us how to build a rock-solid

foundation that can withstand whatever the world hurls at us. We want to be faithful in the little things—help us with that today.

Day 2

Memorize Matthew 25:21. As a mom, you are responsible for so much. Your responsibilities just multiplied when you became a part of a blended family. The awesome thing is that you have a God on your side that will guide you and help you every step of the way. Go forth, faithful servant!

Day 3

You obviously want a strong family because you have this book. Well, here is how to get that: God and time! God will definitely lead your family as you cling to Him, seek Him and walk in obedience to Him. Time will also help build your family stronger. Think about it… when you are so busy with work, volunteering, day to day chores, errands, etc., where is the time needed to actually develop lines of communication, respect, love—family? Today you are to reevaluate your life. If you don't have the time to just sit down in the evenings and be available for the children to visit with you, or come to you with questions on homework, or read a book together, or share a pint of ice cream… then you are just too busy!!! I encourage you to de-clutter your life. You don't have to be on every committee at church. You don't have to volunteer at every school function. Learn to say "NO!" If you want a closer relationship with God, spend more time getting to know Him and being with Him. If you want a closer relationship with your husband, spend time with him and learn more about him. Your family? I think you have the picture!

Day 4 Through Sacrifice comes Blessing

Today is the day to downsize your outside commitments and activities and obligations. You need time for your husband, the kids, and (don't forget…) YOU! Resign. Delegate. Take a hiatus. Remember, you can be replaced! The committee will survive without you. The event will go on even if you are not there. As a result, your family will survive better… with you. Things will go smoother in your home… with you. God will be pleased… with you!

Day 5 Your Thoughts and Prayers

_____
_____
_____
_____
_____
_____

WEEK 9

Day 1

Therefore, as God's chosen people, holy and dearly loved, clothe yourselves with compassion, kindness, humility, gentleness and patience. Bear with each other and forgive whatever grievances you may have against one another. Forgive as the Lord forgave you. And over all these virtues put on love, which binds them all together in perfect unity.

Colossians 3:12-13

Pity party! It's my book and I'll cry if I want to! My step daughter just checked herself into a psychiatric facility so that her medications could be adjusted. The punch is that she just decided to do this and her three small children were suddenly my responsibility. Yes, I love them. Yes, I "inherited" them when I married Dan—but I still have kids of my own—a husband, home… life! Go ahead and think I'm as hard hearted as they come—but at some point I want this 25 year old to see the bigger picture and quit assuming others will pick up the pieces from her decisions. Okay, compassion is not my strong suit. I was raised to be strong and self sufficient and I guess I expect that in both my biological daughter and my step daughter.

As I let my bitterness out—my heart begins to speak to me (I am surprised Jesus can get a word in edgewise.) I am remembering how my step daughter has a mom with emotional issues; she saw many marriages and divorces throughout her childhood—on both parents' sides; and that she has come a long way since her dad and I married. She restored her first marriage; is a great mom; doing well in school and is a sweet loving daughter. Just because she needs some help right now is no reason for me to think the world is ending!

Reading today's verse makes me ashamed—how sad that I didn't want to "bear" my step daughter's struggle with her. How sad that I didn't "clothe" myself in the very virtues I am trying to instill in her. I am human—you are human. Let your bitterness, anxieties and temper tantrums out to God. Believe me, He is big enough to take it. Then when you have exhausted yourself from venting, He will speak to your heart and gently, lovingly remind you of who you are in this family and what you need to do to provide for them, nurture them, care for them and love them.

> Lord, forgive me for being stubborn. Thank you that you let me vent and then whisper your Word

into me. Thank you that I'm not in this family on my own—but that you are with me all the way.

Day 2

Memorize Colossians 3:12-13. I love the mental picture from these verses. When I get dressed, I put each piece of clothing on deliberately. Each piece has a place. I urge you to "dress" yourself with the characteristics in these verses. Dress deliberately and put each "one" on in the right place.

Day 3

I love making lists. Actually, I love crossing stuff off my lists! It gives me such a sense of accomplishment. I'd like you to make a list today. This list will contain the names of people that you have not shown compassion, kindness, humility, gentleness, patience, or forgiveness to. You may want to limit the time frame, let's say, to within the last year. Take the day to ponder over this.

Day 4 Through Sacrifice comes Blessing

Get your list from yesterday. You may need to pray for God to help you forgive someone in your past who has hurt you. You may need to ask for forgiveness for being rude, harsh, and cold to others. Ask God to 'clean your slate'. Lift every name on your list up to God and ask Him for another chance to be kind, patient, humble, compassionate, gentle, and forgiving today.

Day 5 Your Thoughts and Prayers

WEEK 10

DAY 1

Your Father knows what you need before you ask Him.

Matthew 6:8b

"Confessions of a Step-Mom"

Lord, I can't deal with my own kids—and You saw fit to 'embellish' my life with more responsibility! There is more to pick up, more chauffeuring, more mentoring, more guiding, more encouraging, more disciplining…. AARGH!!! Why me?

The above is an actual journal entry from one of my more selfish moments. My entry also includes a poem that was sent to me via e-mail at that same time. It is amusing to me how God blesses us with tidbits of encouragement along the way when He knows we are trying. I hope the poem blesses you and makes you rethink where you are in life and the situations you are in… and praise God!

> "I asked for Strength…
> and God gave me *difficulties*
> to make me *strong*.
> I asked for Wisdom…
> and God gave me *problems*
> to *solve*.
> I asked for Prosperity…
> and God gave me a *brain and brawn*
> to *work*.
> I asked for Courage…
> and God gave me *obstacles*
> to *overcome*.
> I asked for Love…
> and God gave me *troubled people*
> to *help*.
> I asked for Favors…
> and God gave me *opportunities*.
> I received *nothing I wanted*—
> but I received *everything I needed*."

Author Unknown

Lord, I trust You know what You are doing. Thank You for placing this responsibility on me—You obviously know I can handle it! Thank you for continuing to mold and shape me into a godly woman—even using this blended family to help do that. I continue to pray for Your guidance to be just what my husband and my family need.

DAY 2

Memorize Matthew 6:8b. Rest in this knowledge today.

DAY 3

Journaling is not something I consistently do. There have been various times in my past, though, when I have written down my prayers in a journal. When I take some time to read back through these journals, I am amazed at how God carried me through. If you do not journal already, plan today to get yourself a prayer journal. Then you need to think about what time of day and where would be best to journal. You may be able to journal every day. If not, please set aside at least one time a week—just as in this book—to capture your thoughts and prayers on paper. Down the road, you will be able to have evidence of where you were in your life at the time, and see for yourself how God has moved you forward!

DAY 4 THROUGH SACRIFICE COMES BLESSING

Yes, it is something else to add into your already busy routine. However, when we spend time with God, it is never time wasted! Break in your new journal and get writing!

DAY 5 YOUR THOUGHTS AND PRAYERS

WEEK 11

Day 1

> Their treasures of silver will be taken over by briers (weeds), and thorns will overrun their tents.
>
> Hosea 9:6b

I truly appreciate weed killer. We live on almost two acres, and I have put concrete, a pool, and rock (with weed blanket underneath) to prohibit any little stubborn weeds that might choose to stick their heads up! When one of the little demons does make it through to the top, you can be sure to see me with my handy-dandy three gallon weed killer sprayer. Oh, I keep close watch. When we first moved here, there was nothing but weeds. After much backbreaking labor and a ton of sweat, we finally managed to have something that actually looks like a front and back yard with landscaping … and I'm not going to let it slide back into ruin on my watch!

Your blended-family landscape is a fertile "breeding ground" for weeds, also known as sin. And just as weeds come in all kinds and varieties, so does sin. All it takes is an unkind word to or from your husband. Your children bring a whole new generation of "weeds" to the landscape—and it seems they are more resistant to "weed killers". Then we have your step-children with growing weeds of "Well, you're not my real mom!" Your blended-family landscape must be very carefully nurtured, watered, fertilized (yes, discipline can be an icky, smelly job!), pruned, and weeded. The bright side is that well-tended landscapes yield the most beauty!

> Lord, please help me to use Your tools, prayer and Your Holy Word, to keep the 'weeds' out of my family so that we can 'grow' a family of stability, longevity, security, and love.

Day 2

Memorize Hosea 9:6b. This is part of a verse describing Israel's punishment for not walking in obedience to God. I believe that the lesson here is very clear; God is God and He will do *whatever* it takes to bring us back to Him. Today, think about the treasure of your family and the positive things working within your home.

Day 3

Make a list of the "weeds" that you see are causing problems and ugliness in your family. Spend a little time today giving this list to God and asking Him for the right "weed killer" to remove these sins from your family.

In Song of Songs 2:15, instead of weeds ruining the marriage garden it refers to foxes ruining the vineyards that are in bloom. Foxes, weeds, mold, mildew, grease or grime... *get rid of them!*

DAY 4 THROUGH SACRIFICE COMES BLESSING

Okay, I may just be crazy, but I want you to go outside and find some weeds to pull. Yes, really! For me, it doesn't take going very far. As hard as I try, there are still many different kinds of weeds in my front and back yards. You may need to stop by a park for a few moments. I try to pick some weeds around my church periodically. Be aware of the different kinds you will see when you truly begin to look for them. Remember, your family is the same way. Unfortunately, most of the time we just don't want to look for the little sprigs of sin that pop up here and there. The longer they stay, though, the harder they are to get rid of. Maintaining your "marriage garden" and "family garden" are labor intensive jobs. Find a good "weed killer", (God's Word and prayer), and get busy!

DAY 5 YOUR THOUGHTS AND PRAYERS

_____
_____
_____
_____
_____
_____

WEEK 12

Day 1

> Three times I pleaded with the Lord to take it (a thorn in Paul's flesh) away from me. But he said to me, "My grace is sufficient for you, for my power is made perfect in weakness."
>
> II Corinthians 12:8-9a

I can so relate to Paul. After marrying Dan, I kept praying that his daughter would move out and his son would go live with his mom. These kids were my 'thorns'. (Let me take a sentence to clarify that Paul's thorn was a messenger of Satan—I don't believe my step children are that!)

My prayers are sometimes wrong. God, as my loving Father, hears me, pats me on the back and tells me to "go try again". He is not telling me to pray the same things over again (although there are cases where we need to keep diligently praying the same thing), but to pray for Him to be able to work in me... not the situation I'm in.

I made our family dynamics a mountain. I let resentment creep in which turned into bitterness—and I even let it form a wedge between Dan and me. This "unyielding" can bring evil and that can certainly be a 'messenger of Satan'.

Something had to give! I knew that Dan's children needed to see a solid marriage and have a secure family setting in which they would be nurtured and grow. So God gave me the 'light bulb' moment. Years ago, I sang in a trio and we did a song by FFH entitled "Lord Move, or Move Me". God brought that song back to me during my time of resentment.

> Lord move in a way that I've never seen before, because there's a mountain in the way and a lock on the door. I'm drifting away—waves are crashing on the shore—so Lord move—or move me.

These words just washed over me and my prayers changed. I have learned that when God doesn't change the situation, He wants to change me. I also have the knowledge that through "mountains", "locks on doors", and "thorns", His grace is sufficient for me.

> Lord, You obviously allowed our marriage and family blending. Difficult? Yes! We both bring a different set of 'struggles' to the marriage. But I also know that you either want us to conquer the

'mountains' and 'locks' and 'thorns' or You want to use these obstacles to change us so that we can be victorious in You. Thank You, God, that your Holy Spirit provided the words of this song as a balm to my heart and that I would allow You, once again, to mold, shape, and guide me to be the woman You want me to be.

Day 2

Memorize II Corinthians 12:8-9a. If you have been praying about a situation and are getting frustrated that God hasn't done anything yet, maybe you need to change that prayer. Maybe He wants to move you instead of the "mountain".

Day 3

I want you to find the FFH song, "Lord Move, or Move Me." You should be able to download it on your computer, or call your Christian radio station and ask them to play it, or find the CD entitled "Found a Place" in which it is on. Let this just wash over you. I pray that you will be humbled and awed by God through this song.

Day 4 Through Sacrifice comes Blessing

Spend some time today in prayer turning over situations to God that you have been asking Him to change. Remember the song from yesterday, and be willing for God to do a mighty work in your own heart and life!

Day 5 Your Thoughts and Prayers

WEEK 13

Day 1

> Let us consider how we may spur one another on toward love and good deeds. Let us not give up meeting together, as some are in the habit of doing, but let us encourage one another—and all the more as you see the Day approaching.
>
> Hebrews 10:24-25

These verses are referring to the fact that it is easier for believers in Christ to stay strong in the faith when they are constantly looking for ways to encourage and meet with other believers. These verses can also apply to our families.

We get up in the mornings and turn on the morning news only to be bombarded with bad news. We read the newspaper and find more bad news. Our kids go to school and hear and see a lot of 'bad news.' We go to work and are hit with problems and challenges—we question the integrity of others, their words and their work...more bad news. There has to be a place, for us and our loved ones, that is a safe refuge AND where "good news" is heard! There is—and it is your home. Now, I know that at times our homes can feel more like war zones, but the goal is to create an environment where your family can come and dust off the 'dirt' of the world and replace that with love and support.

When our families first blended, it was like an oil and vinegar mixture—when things were not 'shaken up', the two liquids never mixed. We were just content to stay lying around doing our own thing. So Dan and I implemented "Family Night". We decided that Sunday evening would be the time when we all came together to watch a movie, play a game, or just hang out for a bit. We also made this mandatory.

This was quite humorous at first. There would be some of us that didn't like the movie choice … and so we would sulk. There would be times that other social engagements had to be missed out on … and so we would sulk. Then it got to the point that I didn't want to hang around other people that were sulking…. so I would sulk!

Through Dan's diligence (remember, I was sulking), he kept "shaking up" our family and over time (okay, over a year), we came to resemble a nice vinaigrette! Yes, we were beginning to mix! We started hearing laughter; we even started conversing with each other.

Now the kids ask if they can bring friends over. My daughter's boyfriend asks us what is happening for Family Night and joins us. We have found common ground—a place to find acceptance and love. I'm hoping that this will spur our kids to do the same when they have families of their own. We are not just living for today, but showing our kids how to have a successful future—no matter how the "mix" looks!

> Lord, Your Word is alive and it breathes into us a newness everyday. Help me to breathe You in, to let Your Words run through my heart and mind and, in turn, let that newness be a part of my blended family. Help me to 'shake up' this group so that we find humor, joy, comfort, encouragement, and most importantly, love and acceptance.

Day 2

Memorize Hebrews 10:24-25.

Day 3

Remember to keep shaking things up in your family! Plan something fun to do this coming weekend. It doesn't have to take all day, but the benefits can last a lifetime! Also, you have a second assignment. (I was a teacher for a couple of years!) I want you to call a girl friend, or a co-worker, or a neighbor, and plan an outing. I just went to a movie with a couple of girlfriends. What an enjoyment! Yes, I am wife, mom, homemaker, worker, etc, but I think we sometimes forget that we thrive on our "sisters"!

DAY 4 THROUGH SACRIFICE COMES BLESSING

I don't know how much a sacrifice it will be for you to carry out the "sister" assignment from yesterday, but go do it! By the way, I like Toffee Nut Lattes!

DAY 5 YOUR THOUGHTS AND PRAYERS

_____
_____
_____
_____
_____
_____

WEEK 14

Day 1

There is a time for everything, and a season for every activity under heaven: a time to weep and a time to laugh…

Ecclesiastes 3:1, 4

This book was written for blended-family moms, but I feel it is important to address other issues that can surely pop up in our lives. The following is my heart in a journal entry about my mom.

> My mom has Alzheimer's disease. I feel like I am going to lose her twice—first mentally, and then to death itself. I feel responsible to help my dad with as much as possible—especially by taking mom out for little trips so that he can have some time to himself. I am still having a hard time grasping this change in life—in hers and in mine. I want to help, and yet the

little girl in me still wants her mommy to be there to listen to the problems in my life and to comfort and give advice. I guess it is my time to grow up.

I shared this new phase in my life with my counselor. I told her how selfish I felt and that I was scared about being needed more by my parents. I was ashamed of my attitude of dealing with my mom's disease as being a chore or burden. My sweet counselor told me to just look at this as an opportunity to serve God and honor my parents. She also told me to look for God's blessings through this difficult time. I left that session with a feeling of optimism, ready to take on the problems of the world and looking for God's blessings to be interspersed throughout.

The next time Mom and I went shopping was so much better. I was keeping our conversation light and easy. (Dad felt that she was not ready to know about her condition, so talking about it is just not done.) But at one point, I wanted to push our conversation deeper so I asked her how her new medication was working. She adamantly told me it was working really well. Then she stopped and looked at me and said, "Now why am I taking this medicine?" I told her it was for her short-term memory. She then said, "Well, it doesn't look like it's working too well." We both just broke out in laughter. After I dropped her back off at her home, I thanked God for seeing a blessing.

I believe that my mom knows that she is losing her memory but I cherish the fact that she can still find humor in the situation. Seeing that beautiful quality in her makes me want to live my life that way also. There will be tough times, times of weeping, and yet, times of joy and peace interlaced with the beautiful sound of laughter.

> Lord, when you created us, You gave us a sense of humor and a 'giggle box.' I'm sorry that I haven't used that gift as much as I should have. I know that the people I love and care for everyday especially need to hear the blessings of laughter. So, please tickle my funny bone and fill me with joy that bubbles out in a chorus of giggles!

Day 2

Memorize Ecclesiastes 3:1, 4.

Day 3

Laugh. Find the William Tell Momisms (aka "The Mom Song"), by Anita Renfroe. This song is a must for every mother. The William Tell Overture has just been revived! You can see a preview of it on Anita's website, Anitarenfroe.com., then order it off her website, or see it on Youtube.com. You are gonna need the lyrics to this… it is priceless!

Day 4 Through Sacrifice comes Blessing

Do something funny today. Bake cookies with the kids and have a flour fight! Have a pillow fight! Have a water balloon fight! (I must be feeling aggressive today—I'm obviously looking for a fight! LOL) Oh well, the object is to break the normal, humdrum evening and have the gang giggling! What a sacrifice!!!

DAY 5 YOUR THOUGHTS AND PRAYERS

_____
_____
_____
_____
_____
_____

WEEK 15

Day 1

And my God will meet all your needs according to His glorious riches in Christ Jesus.

Philippians 4:19

I don't usually remember lines from a movie, but in the movie "Evan Almighty" there is a scene that just brought me to a place of amazement. I was pleasantly surprised with this movie and its little 'gems' strewn throughout. Morgan Freeman (God) is talking to Evan's wife (aka Mrs. Noah). She is frustrated with Evan for building this ark and doesn't understand what is going on with him. God, (Freeman), sits down and tells her this:

> If someone prays for patience, do you think God gives them patience
> or does He give them the opportunity to be patient?

> If they pray for courage, does God give them courage or does
> He give them the opportunity to be courageous?
> If someone prayed for the family to be close, do you think
> God zaps them with warm fuzzy feelings or does He give them
> the opportunity to love each other?

As I thought about these lines, God recalled past situations to my mind where I could see this in our own family. Dan and I both wanted a close family and we knew that it would take extra ordinary amounts of faith, love, patience, strength, tolerance, forgiveness, and commitment. We believed that our past experiences would give us an edge on our future. Some of those experiences did help us… but we are finding that when a life lesson needs to be learned, it is usually through experience.

In a time that I needed courage, God "grew" that in me when I had to go to my twenty-two year old step-daughter and set boundaries. I thought I was already courageous, especially after surviving the death of a spouse and seven years of being a single mom, but God used this opportunity not only to set needed boundaries, but to give way to respect.

I have also prayed from the beginning of our marriage that our joined family would be close. The movie lines are right. God doesn't just zap us with these instant feelings.

God has been growing us though. When my step-son was threatened verbally, I had my claws out and was ready to do battle for him. I never even knew when God had instilled that feeling in me. Wow ... God took a nasty situation and brought us closer. As far as patience goes, God is giving me the opportunity to wait for some of them to move out! ; -)

> Lord, thank You for not 'zapping' important qualities and traits into us. You must love us so much to provide us with the opportunities to learn and grow and experience that maturing process. You really did think of everything! Help me to look for opportunities in the challenges that you allow into our lives. I'm learning to look for the new "sprouts" of growth!

Day 2

Memorize Philippians 4:19. Rest in all this verse means to you.

Day 3

Make plans today to either rent or buy the movie "Evan Almighty". If you have it already, you get extra credit! LOL

Day 4 Through Sacrifice comes Blessing

Your sacrifice today involves getting your family to watch the movie "Evan Almighty". Tonight may not work well, but you got the weekend to accomplish this.

DAY 5 YOUR THOUGHTS AND PRAYERS

_____

_____

_____

_____

_____

_____

WEEK 16

Day 1

If I speak in the tongues of men and of angels, but have not love, I am only a resounding gong or a clanging cymbal. If I have the gift of prophecy and can fathom all mysteries and all knowledge, and if I have a faith that can move mountains, but have not love, I am nothing. If I give all I possess to the poor and surrender my body to the flames, but have not love, I gain nothing.

I Corinthians 13:1-3

Do you ever find yourself just going through the motions? You accomplish things. You are praised for your contributions. Your feelings inside you, though, betray the smile on your face and the acceptance of the compliments.

My husband is so good to tell me how well I have bonded with his children. He has also fussed at me for "rolling my eyes" when he gives me compliments about this. I do see wonderful growth in his kids… I understand that I have played a part in that… but what lies in my heart has been haunting me.

I have been somewhat selfish in my motives. You see, the more Dan's kids mature and become independent and get their lives in order, the quicker they will be out from under my roof. Harsh. Truth is painful. I do know that I have a love for his children, but I search my heart for my motive and don't like what I find.

God doesn't allow us to keep running from our wickedness. He has constantly been putting pressure on me to love openly and freely—without reservations or ulterior motives. So whenever I have done something for one of Dan's kids and then received praise for it, there is an emptiness within me that just eats away at me.

When I look deep down, I realize that this is an area of control that needs to be turned over to God. I need to love, serve, guide, give—freely, without expectations or reservations. I need to be joyous that God entrusted me with Dan's children. God knew that I could give something to each of them that they had not received in their younger years. He knew that during difficult times I would be able to be an example and encourager for Dan's daughter. He knew that I would be able to make a bridge of humor to help mature Dan's son.

The sad part of this is that I have been living the last three years thinking that when Dan's kids get their lives in order and move out, then I will be comfortable in my own home. Instead, I have spiraled downward into a depression.

I'm an optimistic person, so periodically I would be happy—but when one of his kids would need me to do something for them, I would sink back down—feeling trapped, bitter and eager for them to just be able to take care of themselves. A victim's mentality.

I don't want to be a "resounding gong or a clanging cymbal". I want what I do on the outside to come from a heart motivated by love. God's greatest commandments are for us to love… love Him first with all we have and then to turn around and love others. I am amazed at how simple He made things and yet how I can mess up this wonderful part of my life which is a gift from Him.

Just because I'm writing this devotional doesn't mean that I have conquered this… but with Christ "all things are possible." I am going to be spending more time praising God for the family I have and laying my motives at His feet—asking Him to change my heart and help me release my control.

What areas are you holding on to? Are your motives pure and selfless? If you are struggling in your blended family, please don't live each day waiting until things change, the kids move out or go live with another parent. Today is precious and then it's gone. You can do this…

> Lord, thank you for loving me—just as I am. Thank you for continuing to 'nudge' my heart to repent of my motives. Help me to embrace my family openly and purely. I do know that without You I am nothing… and without love I gain nothing.

Day 2

Memorize I Corinthians 13:1-3.

Day 3

Are you waiting for life to be better once _____ happens? Please remember the saying, "Today is a gift and that is why it is called the 'present.'" Accept your "present" from God and embrace your family. Go ahead and tell yourself that with this "present", there is a "lifetime service plan", and it is "non-returnable" and "non-refundable"!

Day 4 Through Sacrifice comes Blessing

Embrace your family. Yes, really! Make sure that each member of your blended family receives lots of hugs today. They could be little squeezes as you compliment them on something they have accomplished, or just great big, bear hugs with some tickling on the side!

Day 5 Your Thoughts and Prayers

_____
_____
_____
_____
_____
_____

WEEK 17

Day 1

Fathers, do not exasperate your children; instead bring them up in the training and instruction of the Lord.

Ephesians 6:4

I have a good friend that is married to a man that exasperates his children. In fact, he exasperates his wife as well, but I am going to focus this devotional on the effects his actions have on his kids.

Let me preface the following by stating that this man is a good provider, faithful husband, and he loves his children; but somehow he allowed the negative events of his childhood to take away his joy in living. We all carry tremendous 'baggage' from our past experiences and how we were raised, but most importantly, we need to realize that our past in no way has to reflect how we want our future to look. In this situation, he allowed the past to weigh him down and keep him from seeing the beauty of the life and family that God had granted him.

He 'rules' his home with a type of military style—"I said it—you do it!" Of course, we are to raise our children to be obedient and respectful, but there is a flip side to that coin. Let me explain. This man once asked me how I got my children to be good students and to do chores. He couldn't understand why his children were lazy and had no desire to do their best in school. As openly and honestly as I could, I explained to him that in my opinion, you have to have a balance in your parenting. Yes, we are to discipline, but when a child sees and hears nothing but "do this, do that, you didn't do that right, why didn't you do better," they become belligerent, rebellious—exasperated. I told him point blank that he needed to play with his kids. I also told him that I don't believe we have the right to discipline our children if we don't love/play/spend time with them. A child feels a certain security when they are disciplined—knowing first and foremost they are loved unconditionally. They can more easily accept the discipline and try to understand where they went wrong. When a child hears nothing but negativity all day long… that is all you are going to get out of them at some point. Yes, attitude reflects leadership. This man looked at me and told me that this is something he didn't know how to do. I believe he better try. If not, his children will continue to struggle in many areas of their lives. Since the kids do not see their dad working to improve their home and family life, they are at a loss as to how to work to improve their situations.

My children are absolutely not perfect... but I have raised them with an attitude of "We work hard and then we play hard." (My 16 year old son is having a few challenges with this at present time! He believes that it should be "Mom and Dan work hard and then I play most of the time! We are working on this!) Life is short here on earth but I definitely believe that it doesn't have to be all "drudge and trudge". God made beauty in where we live—we should see it. God made laughter—we should practice using that as much as possible. God made families—we should embrace these precious times and the precious lives entrusted to us.

> Lord, thank you for our kids. Thank You that Your Word instructs us in ways to raise these kids. Help me to instruct and teach my kids with love and laughter today. Help me to use discipline when needed in an appropriate manner—not exasperating my kids, but raising them in a balanced manner that is pleasing to You.

Day 2

Memorize Ephesians 6:4.

This week is especially crucial to the overall well-being of your blended family. Please take the time to work through this along with your husband. The two of you may have already developed a plan for disciplining your/his children. If you haven't, I can't stress the importance of getting one.

Your children need to see unity. If they feel one ounce of dividedness, they will work that little ounce to their advantage.

Dan and I immediately implemented some guidelines for disciplining our children soon after we married. Our children were already in their teens, but I believe these guidelines will work for children at any age.

First, put up a united front. When one of the children misbehaves, it is imperative that you and your husband do not jump immediately and rain down your "judgment and justice". Stop. Tell the child that you are going to discuss this with dad. Go. Talk the situation over and then come up with a discipline that is agreeable to you both and beneficial to the child. Then, *both of you go* and explain to the child why his actions were inappropriate and what the consequences are for those actions. Realistically, there are going to be times when you and your husband are not home at the same time. If the infraction is fairly major, I would suggest waiting until both of you are home to discuss it and then both deliver the consequence. Minor infractions can be handled with "time out" or "take away". "Time out" can be used for toddlers up through teen years. It has been suggested that the child stay in a designated "time out" space one minute for every year that the child is. In other words, if the child is four years old, then he should remain in 'time out' for four minutes. "Take away" works well with children starting around age three or four on up to eighteen. It worked very well for me when my son pulled a stunt and I ended up with his new cell phone for a week.

Secondly, for the first year or so of your blended-family-marriage, either discipline the children together, or I suggest that you *allow the child's biological parent to discipline.* (You both should be there either way.) Resentments can form fast and don't be surprised to hear for yourself, "Well, you are not my real mom!" When my son pulled his stunt, Dan and I discussed the consequence, and then we both went to him and delivered his "sentence"! I talked and Dan was there to back me up. Now that we have been married almost five years, Dan is able to discipline my son as needed when I'm not around. We set the foundation solid!

Day 3

Discuss disciplining your children with your husband and form some concrete guidelines. You may only come up with a couple—maybe the same ones Dan and I chose. I have noticed in my years of marriage—both to Dan and my first husband—that when we are in agreement and working together, the kids "feel" this and are somehow more secure in their home and in their life and in our marriage!

Day 4 Through Sacrifice comes Blessing

Sit down with your children tonight or this weekend and share your disciplining guidelines with them. This family is an awesome, winning team, especially with you and your husband as Co-Captains! Rah!

Day 5 Your Thoughts and Prayers

WEEK 18

Day 1

> I know that there is nothing better for men than to be happy and do good while they live. That everyone may eat and drink, and find satisfaction in all his toil—this is the gift of God.
>
> Ecclesiastes 3:12-13

"Live well, laugh often, love much." I want my life to reflect this motto that is a simple statement about the basics of life—uncluttered. To me, it means knowing our priorities. It reminds us to laugh at life—at ourselves. Finally, and most importantly, it encourages us to love with all we've got I want to take the next ten weeks to really look at what living out this motto would look like. I believe that the motto reflects the verses—be happy, do good, and find satisfaction. Piece of cake!

Live well. We are going to look at five ways to live well, remembering that when one area of our lives becomes unbalanced, it skews up all of the other areas. The first point to living well is to make and take time for God every day. Matthew 6:33 tells us to *"seek first His kingdom and His righteousness, and all these things will be given to you as well."* Living well means starting our day with God and then knowing and believing that because we have set our priorities correctly, He will guide us through the day—providing all that we need. I don't know how this will look for you. It may mean getting up fifteen minutes earlier to come before God and lay your life and your day before Him. You may find it easier to pray and worship God on the way to work during your commute time. I know a friend that has wonderful prayer and fellowship time during her morning shower. That is the wonderful thing about our God—He will meet us anywhere!

Be sure to include God's Word in your day. I am reminded about a prayer that I have heard my dad say many times before a meal, "as this food nourishes our bodies, may Thy Word nourish our souls." Without the Bible, we can become spiritually malnourished. The Bible is our guide, light, instruction manual, which also contains 'warning labels' and examples. It shows us God's mercy, grace, patience, deliverance, discipline, salvation and love.

As a mom in a blended family, your life is pulled from so many different angles. You definitely need an "anchor" to keep yourself grounded. God's Word is your best defense! Read it, study it, memorize it, tape it to your mirror… just get in it!

> Lord, I want to live well. I want my life to reflect a tranquility that only comes from knowing You and being in Your Word. I want to seek You first. Help me infuse my day with moments of praise and worship to You. Help me make You a priority—knowing that You will order everything else in my life.

Day 2

Memorize Ecclesiastes 3:12-13 and Matthew 6:33.

Day 3

Find a Bible study to do today. Your Christian bookstore has a plethora of options or you might find something interesting online. Of course, you always have the Bible itself to read and soak in!

Day 4 Through Sacrifice comes Blessing

Get started on that new Bible study! With God first in your life—your Foundation—you will be able to build a better day upon that!

Day 5 Your Thoughts and Prayers

_____
_____
_____
_____
_____
_____

WEEK 19

Day 1

> I know that there is nothing better for men than to be happy and do good while they live. That everyone may eat and drink, and find satisfaction in all his toil—this is the gift of God.
>
> Ecclesiastes 3:12-13

"Live well, laugh often, love much." We continue to look at the basics of life—focusing in on what it means to live well. Last week, we talked about your first objective in life—to seek God. Your next priority in life is your husband. This may be one of the toughest realignment of priorities you have ever faced. I have definitely been there. Dan has definitely been there. I bet you have been—or are there, too.

After my first husband died, it was just me and the kids for over seven years. The kids were my priority. Things worked well that way. It continued to work well until I married Dan.

My daughter was hit the hardest by my marrying Dan. She had had me at her beck and call for years and now she felt like she was on the back burner. I admit, placing Dan first in my life was difficult but I knew it was the right thing to do. The Bible tells us to cleave to our spouses. Matthew 19:5 says, *"For this reason a man will leave his father and mother and be united (cleave) to his wife, and the two will become one flesh."* At some point, my own children will leave me for their mates. We only get the opportunity to have these precious ones for just a short time under our thumbs. Then they leave… and we experience the "empty nest syndrome". I don't want to look at Dan when that time comes and think, "Who is this man and what do I do with him now?"

Please don't misunderstand me; as moms we want to do all that we can to help our children grow up to be successful, happy, and productive individuals. We want to participate in their lives and offer them opportunities to try different sports and activities, but I believe that we can be 'SuperMom' and still let our husbands and kids know that hubby comes first. Example: Saturday night is date night for Dan and me. I look forward to that time to reconnect—to feel like a teenage girl in love again! Right after we married, the kids just thought that I'd be there for them no matter what or when. Saturday evening came and my daughter wanted to have friends over. I told her that Dan and I were going out and she was not allowed to have friends over without us being home. I thought her world would crash right then and there.

She couldn't understand why we just couldn't go out another night. She wanted us to rearrange our plans around hers. I'm thankful that God helped me to stand firm and let her know that being with my husband was of utmost importance to me on our date night.

I'm happy to report that as she has grown and matured, she totally realizes that what I did was right. She has even told us that she respects that. I believe that the example that Dan and I have tried to set will have life-time implications for her marriage and children.

> Lord, help me today to seek You in all I do and then please help me to make sure my husband knows that he is 'next in line' for my devotion and attention. Help me to balance this with the kids—so that they feel loved and secure and they also know that their dad and I are in love and totally devoted to each other.

Day 2

Say Ecclesiastes 3:12-13 from memory and then memorize Matthew 19:5.

Day 3

Plan a "hot date" with your hubby this weekend. Work together on this and then talk it up in front of your children.

You might even want to include lots of hugs and kisses in front of the kiddos to gross them out!

DAY 4 THROUGH SACRIFICE COMES BLESSING

I don't know how much of a sacrifice this will be, but go enjoy that hot date with hubby! Be sure to let hubby know that he is a priority in your life.

DAY 5 YOUR THOUGHTS AND PRAYERS

_____

_____

_____

_____

_____

_____

WEEK 20

Day 1

I know that there is nothing better for men than to be happy and do good while they live. That everyone may eat and drink, and find satisfaction in all his toil—this is the gift of God.

Ecclesiastes 3:12-13

"Live well, laugh often, love much." Simplification, balance, and knowing your priorities—these are the basics of a life without stress. As we continue looking at our priorities, the next one is your family. We start with God, then move to our husbands and then on to our families.

I am at a point in my life where I am still trying to raise kids and help more in my parents' lives. This takes time and effort. When I look back on my past efforts, though, I find a smile creep across my face. Taking time—making time—is really easier than you think. It all starts with a plan—a commitment. I decided awhile back that I needed to go over to my folks' house for a morning visit and coffee once a week. I picked a day that would work for us both and then set it in stone. Those have been good visits that have provided time for us to connect into each other's lives. They appreciate me showing my love to them by just being there. I appreciate them for all the years they have loved me. I guess you could call it a "mutual admiration society"! I wish that spending time with my 16-year-old son was as easy! He doesn't seem to follow a set time or pattern of wanting to connect with Dan and me. We just have to be ready and willing to engage with him whenever he shows any interest of giving us the time of day! Those times are good too. I find that when we are there for him—whenever—he is much more willing to open up to us on a more regular basis. I try different things to allow opportunities for him to share his day and thoughts with me. When he comes home from school, I sometimes have a snack ready for him. It's funny how food seems to open up a conversation with him! I have just recently decided that on Fridays I would take him a lunch (from his choice of fast food places) and eat with him at school. At first, I figured he would be embarrassed to have his mom eat with him at school. He truly surprised me. We talked, laughed, ate and then he hugged me when it was time to leave! I got a hug from him—in public! Wow!

Oh sure, I have lots of other things that I could be doing besides having coffee and donuts with my folks or taking time to eat lunch with my son at school. Somehow though, I can't think of anything else that would make more of an impact on our lives. Show your love through prioritizing your family—by being there and just spending time with them. This will give you more of a "return on your investment" than ever imagined.

> Lord, thank You for my family. I pray that today I would take/make time to just be with them—however that needs to look like right now. Help me to show each member of my family that they are a priority in my life. Especially help me to be able to 'connect' with my step children so that they will grow up with a certainty of love and 'belonging' and acceptance from me. Bless this family, Lord. Thank You.

Day 2

Say Ecclesiastes 3:12-13 from memory. Memorize Proverbs 31:28.

Day 3

Think about Proverbs 31:28 today. What would this Proverbs woman look like in your home? Probably one way to get my son to call me "blessed" would be to sit down at the piano with him and have a jam session. It sometimes is really just that easy.

Day 4 Through Sacrifice comes Blessing

Make time to just 'be' with your children. Silence your cell phone, turn off the TV, and shut down the computer. Play "Go Fish", hopscotch on the sidewalk, lay on the grass and count the stars, make a fort in your living room with blankets and sheets, take a drive to someplace scenic, etc. Get ready to watch hearts bond and family ties strengthen!

Day 5 Your Thoughts and Prayers

_____

_____

_____

_____

_____

_____

WEEK 21

Day 1

> I know that there is nothing better for men than to be happy and do good while they live. That everyone may eat and drink, and find satisfaction in all his toil—this is the gift of God.
>
> Ecclesiastes 3:12-13

"Live well, laugh often, love much." Continuing to dissect this motto, I want to talk to you more about prioritizing—I want you to prioritize YOU!

I spoke at a ladies retreat some time ago on the subject of love. As I researched this topic, a particular verse just kept coming back to me. In Matthew 22:37-39, Jesus is replying to a Pharisee regarding what the greatest commandment is. Jesus tells him, "Love the Lord your God with all your heart and with all your soul and with all your mind. This is the first and greatest commandment. And the second is like it: Love your neighbor as yourself." It seems logical for us to place God first in our lives and then love others—our neighbors—those that are in our lives and around us. But it is the last part of verse 39 that caught me… to love our neighbors as we are to love ourselves. As moms, women, wives, we seem to forget about loving ourselves. We are so busy trying to meet everyone else's needs that most of our own needs go unmet. For me, this is quite visible to the outside world. I have been so busy trying to blend this family and deal with all the emotional issues that come with death, divorce and now regrouping, that my body is what takes the toll. Before I married Dan, I was on the treadmill every day and eating a fairly healthy diet. Then the many different issues of a blended family hit me. Of course, the first thing to go was the exercise. I was so busy struggling with all my internal emotions along with the challenges of setting boundaries, nurturing, and trying to love this newly formed family that thoughts of taking care of me were almost nonexistent. Well, after gaining eighty pounds, I realized that I was not living God's greatest commandments to us. When you are not healthy, you truly have a hard time loving God and loving others. You're tired, have a low self esteem, which in turn for me, lead to depression. This is where I had to make a decision. So many things were at stake. My physical abilities were hindered. My intimacy with Dan was overshadowed by embarrassment. My attitude became negative.

Then I started loving myself again. I'm now at the gym almost every day. I am reducing my food portions and choosing healthier foods. I am pampering myself periodically by getting my nails done and taking relaxing baths with lavender bath salts. This may not be your "cup of tea", but you need to find ways to take care of you! I want to give the best to my husband and family... that means that I need to give them the best of me!

> Lord, I know there are areas in my life where I have neglected myself. I know that in order to be truly effective as your witness, as a wife, mom, and all the other 'hats' that I wear, I need to be healthy. I need to be a priority. I pray that You would help me to make/take time for myself.

Day 2

Memorize Matthew 22:39. Say Ecclesiastes 3:12-13 from memory.

Day 3

Oh, you are gonna love this! Your homework for today is to plan to pamper yourself this weekend. Pedicures, waxes, haircuts, "oh my"! Massages, manicures, milkshakes... well maybe not the milkshake!

Day 4 Through Sacrifice comes Blessing

Please make sure you follow through with your plans from yesterday and "sacrifice" yourself! LOL I also want you to go ahead and plan on doing something to pamper yourself at least once a month. Not only are you worth it, but your family ends up winning too!

DAY 5 YOUR THOUGHTS AND PRAYERS

_____
_____
_____
_____
_____
_____

WEEK 22

Day 1

> I know that there is nothing better for men than to be happy and do good while they live. That everyone may eat and drink, and find satisfaction in all his toil—this is the gift of God.
>
> Ecclesiastes 3:12-13

"Live well, laugh often, love much." I believe that when we have our life ordered, there is a certain calm and peace that just flows from us. We know that God needs to be first in our lives, then our husbands, then our family and last but not least on the list, YOU! The last priority that I want to share with you is the priority of keeping up your home and being organized. I am aware that most of you have jobs outside of the home. I am aware of the tremendous time that it takes to clean a house and get it organized. You may be thinking, "There are not enough 'Merry Maids' on the planet to get my house clean and organized." Hear me out… I have a good reason for listing this as a priority to living well.

I Timothy 3 talks to us about overseers and deacons. I want to look at verses 4-6; "He must manage his own family well and see that his children obey him with proper respect. (If anyone does not know how to manage his own family, how can he take care of God's church?)" Also, in verse 12 it says, "A deacon must be the husband of but one wife and must manage his children and his household well." I'm certainly not a deacon or an overseer in the church, but I am an overseer of my family and home. If I cannot manage my own family and home, how could I possibly be effective in the outside world? God has given me immediate responsibilities—taking care of the "inner circle". When I go through my days knowing that my husband is respected and taken care of; when I have taken the time to be with my kids and listen to them and be involved in their lives; when I have taken care of my body and taken time for me; when I have my home neat and picked up; when I know that in case I need a hammer, three-hole punch, Hawaiian leis, (or whatever), I can go right to where they are—that is managing my family and home well. Knowing that my husband, kids, I and my home are taken care of gives me the clearness of mind to go outside of my home to minister to someone else or tackle an outside project. When I let the house run down, or the laundry pile up and nobody has taken the time to put things back—that brings about chaos. People get frustrated because things are a mess and they can't find anything. I also think that when you teach your children to clean and pick up after themselves, it teaches them responsibility.

This may be an area that you have already achieved success in. If not, don't worry. You can start today to have a cleaner, picked up, and organized home. This is a journey that you shouldn't take alone! Get the family involved. Remember, the more you get this blended family to "mix it up", the more mixed up it will be! When my kids were little, I would play the game "Ten Minute Pick Up". I would divvy out the chores and then we would all scramble to get as much as we could done. Now, in all honesty, I must tell you that I would do this right before we were going to leave to go do something fun. Bribery does work! I will also tell you that it made coming back home so much more enjoyable. The key to this is getting to a point where you know you are being a good steward of the home that God has given you. Then you just might hear God's voice speak these words to you from Matthew 25:23; "Well done, good and faithful servant! You have been faithful with a few things; I will put you in charge of many things. Come and share your master's happiness!"

> Lord, thank you for the many blessings you have given this family. I pray that You would help me to honor You and honor my family by motivating me to be faithful in keeping a home that is clean, picked up and organized. I pray that as each family member has a part of this process, they will feel more a part of this family. I know You will be pleased and I can share in your happiness!

Day 2

Say Ecclesiastes 3:12-13 from memory. Memorize Matthew 25:23.

Day 3

Operation Organization! The first thing I recommend is a big garbage sack. I keep that in the garage for clothes and shoes that are no longer worn and need to go to a donation center. When the sack gets full, I just drop it off when I'm doing my errands. Next, try to group common things together. For instance, all of our games, cards, and puzzles are kept in one place. I have made a shelf in a closet designated just for those things. I have some storage bins where I keep gift bags and ribbon and wrapping paper. I have made a place for office/school supplies, computer stuff, arts and crafts, etc. Organization keeps chaos out!

This has worked for me. Please draw up your own personal Operation Organization strategy today!

Day 4 Through Sacrifice comes Blessing

Take today or this weekend to carry out your Operation Organization plan. It really is cool to actually know where everything is in your home. Once everything has been sorted and put in its place, then be diligent to keep it that way. This can be tough. I have found, though, that once something is already in my hands, it doesn't take that much more effort to put it back in place. In fact, it saves time from having to come back at a later time and pick it up again and put it up. Empower yourself!

DAY 5 YOUR THOUGHTS AND PRAYERS

_____

_____

_____

_____

_____

_____

WEEK 23

DAY 1

I know that there is nothing better for men than to be happy and do good while they live. That everyone may eat and drink, and find satisfaction in all his toil—this is the gift of God.

Ecclesiastes 3:12-13

"There is time for everything, a time to weep and a time to laugh." Ecclesiastes 3:1, 4a

"Live well, laugh often, love much." As we continue digging deeper into this short motto, I want us to search our hearts to see if we can find laughter. Do we laugh when one of the kids does something silly, or do we immediately scorn them? Do we giggle when someone accidently farts at the dinner table, or do we set our faces into a scowl? I remember some very profound words from my first mother-in-law… "pick your battles"." I would rather laugh about passing gas, and then be able to discipline/correct when something more serious occurs. I have found that laughter can lighten the load. It sets a tone in the home that nothing else can match. So be careful in picking your battles—make sure they are worth the war!

I want my kids knowing that laughing at silliness and at ourselves is freeing! My daughter is somewhat of a klutz and also does and says some pretty funny stuff. We call them Jasa-isms! At first, these situations were terrible and caused much grief. Then we turned those awkward, embarrassing moments into laughter. She found out that when she could freely laugh at herself, others just joined in. She became "cool" at school.

Laughter is a by-product of joy. From a joyful heart, laughter just bubbles up and out. When we seek joy everyday, we open ourselves up to laughter. It is very difficult to be depressed and laugh heartily. I know—I've been there. My husband just encouraged me to find my joy. I would think about my God—His salvation, protection, provision, and plan for my life, the wonderful husband He gave me and the kids He blessed us with, the home He picked for us, the job He opened up for Dan, the church home He lead us both to—even the cats and dogs! When you look for the good in your life, you can come up with quite a list. The same goes for when you look for the negative—so don't even start that list!

Another thing to remember is this: your joy isn't so much derived by who you are… but WHOSE you are! Read out loud these verses found in Psalm 66: 1-4.

Shout with joy to God, all the earth! Sing the glory of His name; make His praise glorious! Say to God, "How awesome are Your deeds! So great is your power that Your enemies cringe before You. All the earth bows down to You; they sing praise to You, they sing praise to Your name."

Lord, let me turn my face upwards to You and also my attitude. Show me the blessings and joys in this family and let those joys bubble into laughter that will spread throughout this home. Use me, Father, to show our children how to "not sweat the small stuff" and be able to laugh at the missteps and mistakes that happen in life.

Day 2

Memorize Ecclesiastes 3:1, 4a.

Day 3

Memorize Psalm 66:1-4. Reflect upon who God is and what He has done in your life.

Day 4 Through Sacrifice comes Blessing

Make a list of the awesome deeds that God has done in your life and in your family's life. As your write each one, praise God for His goodness!

Day 5 Your Thoughts and Prayers

WEEK 24

DAY 1

> I know that there is nothing better for men than to be happy and do good while they live. That everyone may eat and drink, and find satisfaction in all his toil—this is the gift of God.
>
> Ecclesiastes 3:12-13

"Live well, laugh often, love much." What does 'love much' mean? In my estimation, this means laying your heart out for others to step on, stomp on—crush. (and to think I'm an optimist!) I also adamantly believe the words of Shakespeare, "It is better to have loved and lost than to have never loved at all." Oh, how true. There have been good times, growing times, and hard times. Each different passage of time is a vital part of me—strength, maturity, and wisdom. I would have missed out on so much if I had not taken a chance on love. This view of love also helped me to open my heart to

Dan. I confess that we are still working on the "wall" that I put up to protect my heart in case he dies early in life as my first husband did. (Our past certainly seems to hang onto us.) God and Dan have been so patient, loving and gentle that I feel the "wall" coming down and I'm letting myself become more open to Dan—more vulnerable—more able to give and receive love. When you open up your life to others, you open yourself to conflict and hurt. The wondrous flip side to this is that you also open yourself up to the tremendous opportunity to feel alive and vibrant. Your family works the same way. As you open your heart to each new member, you face the possibilities of pain and struggle. You also face the glorious joy that comes from loving and being loved—and that far outweighs the negatives!

Giving and receiving love seems to be our life force. In fact, love is the ultimate goal. Mark 12:29 is the start of a passage where a teacher of the law asked Jesus what the most important commandment is. Jesus responds with these words.

> The most important one is this, "Hear O Israel, the Lord our God, the Lord is one. Love the Lord your God with all your heart and with all your soul and with all your mind and with all your strength." The second is this, "love your neighbor as yourself." There is no commandment greater than these.

Back to the basics—love God, love others, and love yourself. (Sound familiar?) As I deal with my marriage, kids, parents, etc., I am reminded that this verse must play out in my life for any possible chances of success.

God loved you so much that He gave the ultimate sacrifice- His Son—a very part of Himself. He risked it all and took a chance for YOU in hopes that you would come to Him and love Him back. I am ashamed at how many times His heart has felt stepped on, stomped on, crushed—because of my sin. Yet, I think that He believes that it is better to love me and 'gain' my love in return than to have never loved or sought after me at all. Shakespeare had it right!

> Lord, You loved me first. You gave up Your Son for me. You want me to love—You first, and then others and myself. Lead me, Father, in this adventure—risk and thrill. As I take Your commandment to heart, help me start here within my own home. Help me to love much!

DAY 2

Memorize Mark 12: 30-31.

DAY 3

I want you to spend time today loving God. It may be through singing, writing Him a love letter, lifting your hands in worship and declaring praises to Him, or laying prostrate before Him in adoration. However it looks, we are called to love Him first with everything we have. I know God will love receiving your affections.

Day 4 Through Sacrifice comes Blessing

When we take the time and make the effort to love and praise God, the result seems to be that we have more time and love to give to others. Experiment with this. Again, spend time loving God. Then use your own family as guinea pigs and love each one of them. Don't stop there… experiment with the people you come into contact today. Love is so versatile. It comes in the form of a smile, a helping hand, letting someone go ahead of you, a phone call of encouragement, a little note of admiration, a good deed, etc, etc. How many lives can you pour God's love out to today? I think you are going to be amazed!

Day 5 Your Thoughts and Prayers

_____
_____
_____
_____
_____
_____

WEEK 25

Day 1

> I know that there is nothing better for men than to be happy and do good while they live. That everyone may eat and drink, and find satisfaction in all his toil—this is the gift of God.
>
> Ecclesiastes 3:12-13

"Live well, laugh often, love much." I Corinthians 13 is the Love Chapter. Please take the time now to read this chapter and let it sink into your heart. The latter parts of verses one, two, and three strike a nerve with me. Basically, without love we are just a lot of noise; we are nothing; we gain nothing. I don't want that. Love in Christ Jesus is to be the foundation of our lives. Upon that foundation, a life of love and joy can be securely built.

Loving your husband's children may be easy for you. Others of us need a bit of encouragement to "activate" that love. I think that when you break down what loving someone else encompasses, you will find it easier to love than you think.

Drawing from our Love Chapter, starting in verse four, we see that *love is patient and kind.* Be patient with your children. Don't be so quick to rush and get upset for their slowness or clumsiness. Be kind and polite. You are the role model. You set the tone and feel of your home. Make it a place where being helpful and having manners are held in high esteem.

Don't be envious—thank God for your step-children's gifts and talents and then thank God for what He gave yours! They have all been masterfully crafted and created by God. Find ways to appreciate their originality.

Love does not boast and is not proud so don't go "tripping" over yourself! (Pride goeth before a fall!) *"Therefore, as it is written: 'Let him who boasts boast in the Lord.'"* I Corinthians 1:31

> Lord, as I dissect this word, *love*, help me to place its components into action. I pray that Your Holy Spirit would open my eyes for opportunities to be patient and kind. I ask that You would forgive me if I have been envious, boastful, or proud. Instead, please help me to see Your artistry in each child that You have placed in my care and boast about Your goodness to this family.

Day 2

Memorize 1 Corinthians 13:4.

Day 3

Patient, kind, not envious, not boastful, not proud. Where do you stand with the first five aspects of love? Spend some time reflecting about this today and see if there are some areas that you could improve upon.

Day 4 Through Sacrifice comes Blessing

If you found some areas of love that you struggle with, I challenge you to sit down with your husband and talk about it. Then, pray together. Ask God for His help in these areas. Who knows? This may open up an opportunity for your husband to share some of his own struggles with you!

Day 5 Your Thoughts and Prayers

_____
_____
_____
_____
_____
_____

WEEK 26

Day 1

I know that there is nothing better for men than to be happy and do good while they live. That everyone may eat and drink, and find satisfaction in all his toil—this is the gift of God.

Ecclesiastes 3:12-13

"Live well, laugh often, love much." Read I Corinthians 13 again. We want to learn to "live" the word love and not just speak it. Today we will start with verse five: *Love is not rude.* This is another problem area for me. It is so much easier for me to have a harsh verbal comeback rather than hold my tongue. Philippians 1:27 tells us to conduct ourselves in a manner worthy of the gospel of Christ. Ouch! Maybe I should carry a clothes pin around with me to remind me to keep my trap shut!

Love is not self-seeking. Our world is so into self gratification—on the spot. No wonder we live in such a lost place. We are not to live our lives in search of pleasing ourselves, but to serve others and to want the best for others. Most importantly, we were created by God—for God. That is why we find fulfillment in service—not self. We are told what we are to seek in life; "But seek first His kingdom and His righteousness, and all these things will be given to you as well". (Matthew 6:33)

Love is not easily angered. Keep your cool! Things happen, mistakes are made, and accidents occur. You have been forgiven much, so return the favor! Proverbs 29:22 tells us that "An angry man stirs up dissension, and a hot-tempered one commits many sins." Anger and rage can most often make a situation worse. The goal is to define the situation or problem and then seek solutions, forgiveness, and healing. Remember, when you add lighter fluid to a fire, you risk being burned, singed and scarred. Our blended families are fragile—don't do irreparable damage with your anger.

Love does not keep records of wrongs. Don't record your children's mistakes or remind them of past failures. Each day keep hoping for the best. When mistakes are made, gently correct and then expect the best. So many times our kids will live up to our expectations!

Love does not delight in evil but rejoices in the truth. Be truthful. When your family blended, there were difficulties and there probably still are. Be honest. This joint venture is going to have many ups and downs. Sharing your heart with each other will help everyone in your family be able to have a better understanding of where your family is and where you want it to go. Zechariah 8:16a says, "These are the things you are to do: Speak the truth to each other."

> Lord, help me to continue to break down the components of the word **love**. Today I commit to You to hold my tongue, look for ways to serve others, let go of my anger, not fling past mistakes of others into their faces, and speak the truth in love. I want to be the godly mother that this family needs and I know that starts with leading by example. I know that "I can do all things through Christ who strengthens me." Thank You for loving me and giving me Your Word and Your precious Son's example.

Day 2

Memorize 1 Corinthians 13:4-6.

Day 3

Let's evaluate the next four aspects of love. It is not rude, not self-seeking, not easily angered, doesn't keep record of wrongs, and is truthful. Is there an area or two (or three?) that you need to turn over to God and ask for forgiveness and help? God is so eager to help you. He wants to continue to mold and shape us into the image of His Son, Jesus. That means you have to acknowledge your sins and pivot from that old direction into a new and better direction.

Day 4 Through Sacrifice comes Blessing

Again, take time to sit down with your husband and share any aspects of love that you struggle with. Sometimes, just confessing our struggles out loud can have a profound impact. Don't forget to pray together.

Day 5 Your Thoughts and Prayers

___
___
___
___
___
___

WEEK 27

Day 1

> I know that there is nothing better for men than to be happy and do good while they live. That everyone may eat and drink, and find satisfaction in all his toil—this is the gift of God.
>
> Ecclesiastes 3:12-13

"Live well, laugh often, love much." Read I Corinthians 13 again. This is the last week we will look at this chapter for our definition of the word *love*. I hope you are recognizing areas of strength within our search. I also hope you see areas that are screaming for change. You are obviously reading this devotional as a tool to help you become a better blended-family mom. So then, take those areas of love which are troublesome and give them to God. It is only when we acknowledge our faults and struggles that we can begin to overcome them. Love is a big word—thank goodness we can learn to love a facet at a time!

Love always protects. Being a part of any relationship requires protection. When we are entrusted with personal information regarding another, we need to guard that information dearly. Once again, this is not one of my better areas. I admit that when one of my kids does something wrong or stupid, one of my best friends knows it almost immediately. The problem with this is that my friends now have a tainted view of the child. My philosophy of "living out loud" should pertain to me. My children should have the right of deciding to "live out loud" on their own. My job is to guard and protect them. (Where is that clothespin?)

Love always trusts. To trust means to believe in the honesty and the reliability of others. I think this ties in with expectations. The more you trust your kids—believe in them—expect the best from them—the more trustworthy they will become. Oh, they are going blow it from time to time, but when a child knows that his parents believe in him and believe in his dreams and abilities, there are no limits to his success and achievements.

Love always hopes. We want the best for our kids. We hope their future is filled with love, laughter, joy, fulfillment, and a family of their own to torment them as much as they have tormented us! Seriously, I believe in the words I saw in an orthodontist office years ago; "You are never given a dream without being given the power to make it come true." Be sure to tell your children that they can reach their dreams. God places those desires within us so that we can join with Him to do something wonderful!

Love always perseveres. I try to remember this as I ponder how to get through to my 16-year-old son. I can't give up. I agonize over this as I see my mom lose her memory to Alzheimer's. I won't give up.

You have a list of trials and struggles also. Don't give up. God has given us a promise in Hebrews 10:36. *"You need to persevere so that when you have done the will of God, you will receive what He has promised."* I also know that God will not give us more than we can handle. I Corinthians 10:13 says,

> "No temptation has seized you except what is common to man. And God is faithful; He will not let you be tempted beyond what you can bear. But when you are tempted, He will also provide a way out so that you can stand up under it."

Finally, love never fails. We will fail and fall short; others will fail, but we have this thing called love. It cannot be seen or touched, but we look for it every day. We look for it in the eyes of our husbands, kids, parents, and friends. We feel it in the warmth of a hug or a kiss. We stretch ourselves to go above and beyond for someone we love—just as Christ did for us. Jesus said in John 14:12-13, *"My command is this: Love each other as I have loved you. Greater love has no one than this, that he lay down his life for his friends."* Love is having affection for someone else—so much that you are willing to risk yourself. I remember that feeling when my first husband needed a kidney. I felt like I was in first grade—throwing my hand up in the air saying, "Here I am—take my kidney! I know the risks, but I love you and want the very best for you. I'm willing to risk it all—just for you!" Jesus felt that same way about us. I John 3:16 says, *"This is how we know what love is: Jesus Christ laid down His life for us."* He risked it all for you because He loves you and wants the very best for you. That is a love that will never fail.

> Lord, I choose you. You knew all the risks. You love me so much. I know that you want the best for me. Father, I want the best for this family. Help me to protect these precious ones, trust in them, have high hopes for them, and always persevere in whatever situation You allow us to go through. Thank You that You loved us first. Thank You for a picture of perfect love—Your Son.

Day 2

Memorize 1 Corinthians 13: 4-8a.

Day 3

The last five aspects of love: it always protects, always trusts, always hopes, always perseveres, and never fails (always wins). Isn't it interesting that all these aspects of love found in verse seven have the word "always" in front them. This paints a picture of what UNCONDITIONAL LOVE looks like. As a parent, we are to live out this picture to our children. Do your children know that no matter what happens, you will protect them? Do they know that you trust them? Do they know that you have great hopes for them? Do they know that you will persevere through life with them? Do they know that you will always love them?

DAY 4 THROUGH SACRIFICE COMES BLESSING

Speak to your children daily about how you love them so much you would fight giants; love them so much you would trust them with your life; love them so much and have such high hopes for them; love them so much that you will stand by them through thick and thin; love them so much—unconditionally—forever. I am a true believer of speaking positive things over my children. I even speak positive things over myself. Try this. You may want to write what you say on a note card. Whatever you do, just verbalize these aspects of love to your family. Get ready for a whole lotta' love!

DAY 5 YOUR THOUGHTS AND PRAYERS

_____
_____
_____
_____
_____
_____

WEEK 28

Day 1

I lift my eyes to You, the One enthroned in heaven.

Psalm 123: 1

God has a wonderful sense of humor and perfect timing. He uses people, situations and things to help shape and mold our lives. As I have discovered, He even uses poop.

Monday is "Wonder Woman" day. I clean, wash, scrub, dust, vacuum, wipe down, bleach, and sweep almost everything I can in and around this house as well as go to the gym and fix dinner. Several Monday's ago, as I was bringing my "castle" back to its nearly perfect state, I looked out my back window and saw poop. Not just one little mound, but I saw five or six. My thoughts careened between disposing of it myself and having my husband remind his daughter that she promised to clean up after her new little puppy. Well, the thoughts continued pouring into my head: "I bust my bottom to take care of this place! I don't know why people cannot do what they are supposed to do!" Of course, I let these and other thoughts run rampant that morning and that poop affected my whole day! The backyard was 'poopy.' That afternoon with my mom was 'poopy.' I was 'poopy' to my husband.

Tuesday morning. I had Bible study at ten and I had not done the homework for the week yet. So I settled in and tried to do at least a couple of days of homework before I went to class. In those moments, God spoke to me quite clearly— about poop. You see, where your focus is—is what you listen to and hear—which leads to how you feel—ending in what you expect. I could just hear God telling me to look up. Look to Him. There is always going to be people and situations that I can't change or that I will get frustrated with. But when my focus is on God, I find the love, joy, peace, patience, kindness, goodness, faithfulness, gentleness and self-control to deal with others and their poop!

"I lift my eyes to You, the One enthroned in heaven. Like a servant's eyes on His master's hand, like a servant girl's eyes on her mistress's hand, so our eyes are on the LORD *our God until He shows us favor."* Psalm 123:1-2

> Lord, I'm trying to look up! I want to focus on You so hard that I listen for You and can hear You. I want my feelings to be a result of what I trust about You. I want my expectations formed by what I know of You—not of what my external influences are. Lord, thank You that You work through anybody and anything to draw our eyes to You. I see You.

Day 2

Write down and memorize Psalm 123:1.

Day 3

I don't know what the 'poop' is in your life. It could be the toilet seat left up all the time; dirty clothes lying around; dishes with dried food on them from weeks ago. Whatever it is, look up! Seek God when you come across the pitfalls of your day and then calmly seek the person that needs to rectify the situation—or in other words—pick up their poop!

Day 4 Through Sacrifice comes Blessing

Choose today to not dwell on the clutter and messes that can "attack" your vision. Just like yesterday, fix your focus on God and then calmly handle your life's irritants. Your homework is to do this for the rest of your life! LOL

Day 5 Your Thoughts and Prayers

_____
_____
_____
_____
_____
_____

WEEK 29

Day 1

> Where you go I will go, and where you stay I will stay. Your people will be my people and your God my God.
>
> Ruth 1:16b

I love this statement of commitment. This verse is where Ruth tells Naomi, her mother-in-law, that even though both of their husbands had died, and this was her home, she wanted and was willing to go with Naomi wherever she went. Is someone else so impressed with your life that they would be willing to give up their home or job to follow you and go wherever you go? At a Women of Faith Conference in Dallas, Texas, Patsy Clairmont, my favorite speaker, said something that changed my heart and perspective. She asked if we were living our lives in such a way that our children's spouses could see a difference in the way we live and would want that for themselves. I immediately asked myself if I was living in such a way that my own step-daughter would want to choose my way of living—my God? Does she see the fruits of the Spirit being lived out in front of her every day? Is she drawn to desire Christ through my words and deeds? That gave me cause to pause!

My dad has always been a people person but never pushy or forward with presenting his faith verbally. One day, as he was working, a young man came up and asked what was different in his life. The man saw something that drew him to my dad. Dad didn't talk about church or God at work, but his life quietly reflected it. My dad talked to this young man and shared his faith in Christ as well as the importance of being connected to a body of believers through a local church. We later found out that this young man started attending a church along with his girlfriend. This man wanted what my dad had and was willing to "follow him". This man saw Christ in my dad and wanted what he saw!

Dad didn't have to preach anything. His life reflects honesty, diligence, hard work, patience, love, joy, kindness, and so many other wonderful qualities…. His life reflects Christ. Naomi must have reflected so many beautiful qualities as a wife, mother, and mother-in-law. Ruth was a smart, young woman and recognized that Naomi had her struggles, but she also had something of great importance—a faith in the One True God, our Savior. Ruth saw, first hand, Christ living in and through her mother-in-law. Ruth wanted that also.

Are you allowing Christ to live and work through you? This is the perfect opportunity to affect the lives of your family. If your life isn't "speaking" to those around you, maybe it is time for some good soul searching and removing the clutter and obstacles that are blocking those rays of sunshine from God's Son that can pour out of you into the lives of others.

> Lord, what an incredible testimony—to live in such a way that people are drawn to our lifestyle, our peace, freedom, and joy that only comes from knowing You. I pray that You will help me remove barriers that are blocking others from seeing Your presence in my life. I want others to know You and experience life the way You want them to. Help me live so that others will want to choose You!

DAY 2

Memorize Ruth 1:16b

DAY 3

Ruth's devotion to Naomi just speaks volumes to me. Her commitment to family is inspiring. In fact, I believe that our country's lack of commitment to marriages and families is our biggest downfall.

Draw your own line in the sand. Plant your feet firmly on the side of commitment and obedience. When you make a choice to walk in obedience to God and commit to your man, your marriage, your family, you will be blessed!

Day 4 Through Sacrifice comes Blessing

Ruth is a short book in the Bible. Read this beautiful story of trust and devotion and then desire to have a heart like Ruth.

Day 5 Your Thoughts and Prayers

_____
_____
_____
_____
_____
_____

WEEK 30

Day 1

Do not fear, for I am with you; do not be dismayed, for I am your God. I will strengthen you and help you; I will uphold you with my righteous hand.

Isaiah 41:10

"... and what have I done for You, Lord?"

"... is there any eternal 'worthiness' to my efforts?"

As I ask myself the above questions, I realize my list is rather short. I am 45 years old and I have to ask, "What now?" Can I make up for lost time? I want to live with God as my first priority—not my husband, kids, parents, friends, home, or church.

Some things need to fall away—be banished—left behind—forgotten.

Some things need to be embraced—open armed—not holding anything back.

> Some things need to be added to my life—such as righting wrongs, standing up for justice, seeking others to serve, taking the time—no—making the time to help another that is lost, cold, hungry, naked, needy, or hurting. As God upholds us with His righteous hand, we should also be ready to help others so that His love and light are shown to those in need.

I wrote the above thoughts down when my son and I were staying at a mission in San Francisco on Ellis Street. Our church youth group had the amazing opportunity to go and minister to the homeless and Ellis Street is where you will find most of San Francisco's homeless. When you step outside of the front door of the mission, the smell of urine assaults your nostrils. We witnessed drug deals taking place, saw people snorting cocaine, and we were asked for money and food.

I believe that all the participants on that mission trip would tell you, without a doubt, that they realized it is easier than you think to step outside your comfort zone and lend a hand. We shared sack lunches, hot chocolate, and a listening ear. In return we learned about some of these remarkable people and how they ended up on the streets. I am also amazed that some of these people shared their testimonies with us and blessed us tremendously. It was a win-win situation!

There are so many benefits to helping others:
1. It actually helps others!
2. It trains your kids to open their eyes and look for those in need.
3. It takes the focus off your own family's problems and adjustments and promotes bonding.

When I think back to times that I remember our whole family pulling together, the memory is usually linked with either a family crisis or someone else's tragedy. During these difficult times, we would band together and see what we could do to help. No one whined or complained—there was someone in need and we had to focus on what could be done to help them.

As I re-ask myself this devotional's first question, "What have I done for You, Lord?", I am disheartened about the little I have to offer my God, and yet there is hope that today there is still time to make a difference in someone else's life as well as my family's life. What better way to blend your own family than banding together to help someone else!

> Lord, I don't want to hide myself because my offering of service is small. Instead, I want to take today and make a difference in someone else's life. Open my eyes to the poor, needy, and downtrodden. Help me to shape and mold my kids to open their eyes and see need and then find a way to take action. Lead us today to make a difference not only in someone else's life, but in my family's also.

Day 2

Memorize Isaiah 41:10. Say this verse whenever you are feeling the fear and disappointment that comes from not only raising a family, but the extra challenges associated with raising a blended family.

Day 3

As the mom in your family, you have a great opportunity to shape and mold the children God has entrusted you with. Start this week by organizing an opportunity to help someone else. Get the kids involved in a garage sale, and then give the proceeds to a family in need. Take the kids shopping for school supplies and donate them to a teacher who has students in need. Keep water bottles in the car so that the kids have an opportunity to offer water to a homeless person. Use these ideas or come up with your own.

Day 4 Through Sacrifice comes Blessing

I'm sure you came up with some good ideas yesterday to make a difference in someone else's life. Now it is time to put the 'work to the word'! Go and watch how God will bless your service not only to someone else—but your own family as well.

Day 5 Your Thoughts and Prayers

_____
_____
_____
_____
_____
_____
_____

WEEK 31

Day 1

Open your Bible and read about Jacob in Genesis 31:3-12. This scripture was the basis for a sermon that my son and I heard in a Chinatown church on the San Francisco youth mission trip that was in last week's devotional. The pastor shared with us some background information about Jacob and then discussed the problems in Jacob's life. First, he had to work seven years for the wife of his dreams, Rachel, only to find on the wedding night that he hadn't married Rachel but had been tricked into marrying her older sister. He then worked seven more years for Rachel. Second, Laban, his father-in-law, was repeatedly cheating Jacob on his wages. Even though Jacob was obviously having a tough season in life, we find four phrases that consoled Jacob and will encourage us also when we find ourselves in a tough season of life.

In verse three God tells Jacob, "I will be with you." God saw Jacob's life and how he was being treated. God reminds Jacob (and us), that He is right with us.

In verse five, Jacob shares the situation with his wives and acknowledges that "the God of my father has been with me." Jacob knew that he wasn't alone and that his path had been guided all along by God. Maybe we should be quicker to voice that our God has been with us!

In verse seven we find that even though Laban had been scheming to cheat Jacob out of wages, Jacob was able to say, "God has not allowed him to harm me." Jacob didn't focus on what Laban had been doing to harm him, but focused on God and verbalized it. Our God is our Protector. He constantly has a watchful eye on us and is aware of everything that is done to us. I believe that we just need to speak truth over ourselves and our families, reminding us of God's control and power over every area of our lives.

In verse twelve God tells Jacob, "I have seen all that Laban has been doing to you." God doesn't turn away from us. There is not a second where He blinks His eyes and misses anything in our lives. There was a time when someone was trying to manipulate me and my life. I was devastated. Thank goodness God was there seeing all of that. I praise Him that out of that dark time, He brought about a precious miracle—the sand dollars! (I can't believe I haven't shared that with you yet!!! I will in the next devotional!) Just as God blessed Jacob for his faithfulness and He blessed me during a time of emotional chaos, He will be there for you, carry you through the troubled times, and bless you mightily!

As a mom—whether single, married, blended, (or even pureed! LOL), we all encounter times of feeling scared, mistreated, cheated, confused, and hurt. I have cried to God about situations that have happened in this family and have had pity parties saying, "This isn't right; it isn't fair!" and "Why is this happening to me?" I guess I need to be quick to remember Jacob's story as well as my own. God tells us the same thing He spoke to Jacob: "I will be with you and I have seen what has been going on." I should be more diligent about saying the same things that Jacob did: "My God has been with me and God has not allowed harm to me." Through all of life, God is here! He won't allow you more than you can handle and He certainly knows absolutely everything going on in your life. I Corinthians 10:13 says,

> No temptation has seized you except what is common to man. And God is faithful; He will not let you be tempted beyond what you can bear. But when you are tempted, He will also provide a way out so that you can stand up under it.

Amen!

The pastor closed the sermon with a reading of "Footprints in the Sand." Let this wash over you as you read it, because we are never alone.

Footprints in the Sand

One night I dreamed I was walking along the beach with the Lord. Many scenes from my life flashed across the sky.

In each scene I noticed footprints in the sand.
Sometimes there were two sets of footprints,
other times there was one only.

This bothered me because I noticed that during the low periods of my life, when I was suffering from anguish, sorrow or defeat,

I could see only one set of footprints.

So I said to the Lord, "You promised me Lord, that if I followed you, you would walk with me always.

But I have noticed that during the most trying periods of my life there has only been one set of footprints in the sand.

Why, when I needed you most, have you not been there for me?"

The Lord replied, "The times when you have seen only one set of footprints, my child, is when I carried you."

Mary Stevenson, 1936

Lord, sometimes I don't have a clue how to be a mom in this family. Our children have needs. How do I meet them all? I never knew that combining our two families would be so much of a struggle at times. I even find myself questioning if it is truly worth it. Forgive me. Please help me to remember the words in the scripture. You are with me. You have been with me from the beginning. You have not allowed harm to me. You have seen what others have done to me. Let me also remember that when I feel that I'm by myself on this journey, You are carrying me!

Day 2

Memorize I Corinthians 10:13. As you memorize this, think about how the word temptation could be interchanged with the word struggle. I believe that God works in all things—temptations and struggles. He's got us!

Day 3

Think about how you respond to the temptations and struggles in your own life. Are you quick to point a finger in blame to someone else? Do you spin emotionally out of control? Take inventory of this today.

Day 4 Through Sacrifice comes Blessing

Yesterday, if you found that your responses to the temptations and trials in your life needs some help, then I want you to memorize the four phrases found in Jacob's story. Fill in the blanks with your own words.

God said, "I will be with you."

Jacob said, "the God of my father has been with me."
Jacob said, "God has not allowed _____ to harm me."
God said, "I have seen all that _____ has been doing to you."

DAY 5 YOUR THOUGHTS AND PRAYERS

_____
_____
_____
_____
_____
_____

WEEK 32

DAY 1

Choose for yourselves this day whom you will serve, but as for me and my household, we will serve the Lord.

Joshua 24:15

Have you ever been backed into a corner, only to realize how deeply convicted you are about something? Have you ever been in a dire situation where you had the possibility of losing something you greatly desired and loved? My "corner" happened to be a beach on Mustang Island, Texas. My choice that day was God or the man I wanted to marry. Here is the story—my story.

I had been a widow for seven years and had hardly dated during that time. Between raising two youngsters and a sorry "dating pool" to fish from, it just didn't seem worth the time. God led me and the kids to Abilene, Texas, where my parents live, and shortly thereafter came the man of my dreams! He was a godly man, committed to Christ, devoted to family, loved music, could even sing, had a good job, and was breathing! Sounded like a winner to me, and I fell in love with him. He found that I was what he had been looking for in a wife, and God seemed to be leading us towards marriage. It was about a month before we were to be married when I was given some information about Dan that was potentially damaging and I felt crushed. Questions swirled around in my head such as, "Do I really know this man?" and "Is he out to hurt me or my kids?" My heart had that same feeling as when my first husband had died—that someone had taken it out of my chest and was ripping it into shreds. The pain was so physical.

It was during this time that I was on Mustang Island on the beach with my children. They were playing in the water and I was struggling with this issue, pacing along the water's edge and just crying. As I continued walking up and down the beach, I saw broken sand dollars everywhere. They had been smashed by the crashing of the waves against the shore. It was during this time that I remember giving everything up to God that day. Through my tears, I told God that I could live without Dan in my life but I couldn't live without Him. I chose God. At that point, I asked God for a sign. I knew that I shouldn't, but I just couldn't keep from asking my Heavenly Father for a solid answer to my dilemma. I asked God to let me find a whole sand dollar if I was to marry Dan. I knew that it was silly, but I was desperate to know His will for me and my children. About 30 seconds later, both of the kids started squealing excitedly. I turned around to see both of them with their hands cupped full of sand—along with bunches of whole, living sand dollars. I asked for one, unbroken sand dollar. God gave me about fifty! I like His math!

I chose God and He blessed me. Choosing Him is not always easy, but when you find yourself in that same "corner", I believe that you will forsake everything else and proclaim to Him that you choose Him!

> Lord, forgive me for thinking that if I choose You, I give up everything else that is important to me. What I need to realize is that when I choose You, You make a clearer path for me. When I choose You, my priorities fall into place. When I choose You, I know without a doubt that I am in Your perfect will and have Your guidance and love. Thank You for "dire situations" and "corners" that bring to light what my first choice should always be—YOU!

DAY 2

Memorize Joshua 24:15. Claim this as your own motto.

DAY 3

How do you choose Christ? What, in your life, reflects making the choice to follow Him? Think about this today. We will work more on it tomorrow.

DAY 4 THROUGH SACRIFICE COMES BLESSING

Make a list of your answers to yesterday's questions. If you need to, please decide today to make the changes necessary to let your life reflect that you choose Christ. Do you need to be more diligent about praying at mealtimes and bedtimes? Could you incorporate Bible story time in the evenings? Do you need to commit to being at church every week and getting involved in serving there? As a mom in a blended family, you need every weapon and tool available to be able to raise your family in a God fearing, successful way. Get busy!

DAY 5 YOUR THOUGHTS AND PRAYERS

_____
_____
_____
_____
_____
_____

WEEK 33

Day 1

> Fathers, do not embitter your children, or they will become discouraged.
>
> Colossians 3:21

Pick your battles. These words were spoken to me by my first mother-in-law. I was relating to her about how many things I couldn't get her son to change. (I was a newlywed with high ambitions of turning him into my perfect mate!) She helped me to realize that if I "picked" and found fault with everything I thought was wrong with Mike, I would eventually "pick" apart my marriage. Instead, she advised me to only pick the biggest areas that needed troubleshooting! I am thankful for her advice.

Those words made an impact in my life, again, when my 16-year-old daughter brought home one of her friends. This girl was on a downward spiral of drugs, alcohol, and promiscuity. My daughter, who is much like her mom, said "we can fix her," and therefore brought this girl into our home for "reconstructive" therapy. So we talked, shared, loved on, and encouraged her. Sometimes things went well for awhile and other times she slipped right back into old, destructive patterns. I was brought to a point where I had to give her an ultimatum—either she straighten up and fly right or I would go to her mother. This seemed to truly hit the mark. A couple of days after that poignant conversation, she called to ask a question. "Mrs. Carpenter, I've not drank or done any drugs or had sex, but are you gonna tell my mom if I smoke?" I joyously told this young woman, "If you can give up all those other things, I'll smoke with ya!" Of course, my husband and daughter just about had a fit, especially since I don't smoke! But my point was to pick the biggest battles. The drugs, alcohol, and sexual promiscuity could have immediate damaging affects on her life. Smoking, at that point, was the lesser of the "evils". I certainly do not advocate smoking—but hopefully you see where I was trying to help this girl. By the way—she has turned her life to Christ and is engaged to a fine, young, Christian man.

There are probably lots of things wrong in your blended family. And if your husband has kids, then you probably feel like they have most of the problems! (LOL) Seriously though, *pick your battles*! When a child is constantly ridden and reprimanded about everything he does wrong, at some point, he will become exasperated, embittered, and just want to give up. Remember the human factor. We are human and entered this world evil. That sets us up for failure right there. But God is in control and He sent a Son to forgive us and to conquer every evil battle that we have or ever will encounter. So find the battle that is the most harmful to your child or family. It could be a lack of communication. It might be that you have a child that lies or is rebellious. Maybe the biggest problem is you—your priorities are out of line. Remember to arm yourself for battle and your best armor is God, His Word, and Your faith in Him. The goal is to win the battle with the least amount of damage!

> Lord, thank You for this family. Thank You for so many wonderful aspects of it. But God, there are some things that are damaging and destructive happening. Lead me, guide me, and help me pick the 'battle' that needs to be addressed now. I don't want to exasperate or embitter this family—my husband or children—but want us to grow closer and become stronger. I pray that you would help me 'arm' myself with Your Word and knowing that You are with me. I'm ready Lord!

Day 2

Memorize Colossians 3:21.

Day 3

I remember having a particularly rough day when my kids were little—after my first husband died. I had ranted and raved at them all day about everything. As I replayed all that I had said to them back in my head, I realized I had not said one good thing to them or about them.

God truly spoke to my heart that evening and I knew that this kind of behavior (mine) needed to stop. My perfectionism and explosive outbursts were tearing down my already fragile family. That was my turning point. My children needed to hear that I loved them no matter what. They needed me to hold them close and make them feel safe. They needed laughter. They needed their victories celebrated and their defeats cushioned. They needed positive words flowing out of my mouth about them. That evening changed a lot for me and them. I was able to give God my anger and rage (probably from dealing with my own grief). I was able to ask God to help me raise my children—since He is the perfect Father! Then I released my stronghold of perfectionism… well… not completely but what is wrong with a clean house!? LOL

Your turn. Mentally play back the things you have said to your children during a day. Has your "blending" added some stress? Do you wince just thinking about some of the things your children have heard coming out of your mouth? Take some time and jot down some things that you have said during the last couple of days to your children. Pray for God to help you pick your battles and then for Him to help you speak positively to them. You are going to see the stress in your home drop dramatically.

DAY 4 THROUGH SACRIFICE COMES BLESSING

For every child in your family, take a sheet of paper and put their name at the top. Now write about five things that are good and positive for each child on their sheet. This may be a characteristic or an achievement or attitude. Catch your children doing something good and then go jot it down on their list. Keep the lists on the refrigerator so that they can see and know that you are finding good things about them and recognizing them!

DAY 5 YOUR THOUGHTS AND PRAYERS

_____

_____

_____

_____

_____

_____

WEEK 34

DAY 1

> … for all have sinned and fall short of the glory of God…
>
> Romans 3:23

I have a family member who struggles with pride. Oh, he doesn't know it, but it is there. He compares his mistakes and bad decisions to others and then rationalizes that his sins are not as bad as others. I know that this fairly new Christian will be "schooled" by the Holy Spirit—as He does with all of us in areas that need adjusting.

I had the opportunity to visit with this young man and shared with him about a sin in my life. I had bought something using a credit card when my husband and I had talked specifically about not using them anymore. I rationalized my want at the time without regard to the myriad of problems I was creating or who I was hurting. Then we compared that sin to the sin of adultery. Strangely enough, adultery can be compared to what I did with the credit card… rationalizing a want without regard to the heartache and problems created. In both cases, it is a condition of the heart—pure selfishness. Somehow we get or put ourselves in situations where we shouldn't be in the first place. I admit it; I should not be trusted with a credit card in my purse without my husband with me. The adulterer in this situation shouldn't have been hanging out with the people they were hanging out with and at the place they were hanging out at.

In John 8:1-11, Pharisees and teachers of the law brought a woman to Jesus that had been caught in adultery. They asked Jesus about stoning her to death for her sin. Jesus answered them in verse 7, *"If any one of you is without sin, let him be the first to throw a stone at her."* The story ends with Jesus telling the woman to go and leave her life of sin. Obviously, the teachers and Pharisees weren't good enough to even pick up a pebble!

The next time you come across someone that has sinned in a way that you think is horrendous, please stop and think about these next two verses. Luke 6:41-42, Jesus says,

> Why do you look at the speck of sawdust in your brother's eye and pay no attention to the plank in your own eye? How can you say to your brother, 'Brother, let me take the speck out of your eye,' when you yourself fail to see the plank in your own eye?

> You hypocrite, first take the plank out of your eye, and then you will see clearly to remove the speck from your brother's eye.

It is so easy to see the sin in others and neglect our own.

Your blended family is a breeding ground for sin. Thoughts of jealousy can run rampant; an attitude of pride can harm; deeds done to hurt others can do great damage. Whether in thought or deed, sin is sin. It is for all our sins that Christ was crucified on a cross—planks or specks!

So how do you try to make a difference in your family? Teach them to worry about their own "planks". Teach them to understand that we will all fail each other—somehow, somewhere in someway. Teach them to cut each other some slack or in other words, show grace. Teach them that in order for us to receive forgiveness, we must also forgive. Teach them to want to be more Christ-like. Teach them that choosing God's ways and walking in obedience to Him means freedom.

> Lord, forgive me of my pride. Help me to remember that we all sin and it was those sins that helped nail your Son to a cross—specks and planks. I ask for Your help in teaching my family about grace and forgiveness.

Day 2

Memorize Romans 3:23.

Day 3

How do children learn how to have grace and forgive others? The answer is *you*! How you live your life at home will be mimicked by your children outside the home. I have tried to always apologize to my children if I have overreacted to a situation, or said something hurtful or done something in error. I do not believe that apologizing diminishes my authority as their mother. I believe it helps my children to see that I am human and will make mistakes but also am respectful of them and their feelings. This is summed up in Ephesians 4:32. *"Be kind and compassionate to one another, forgiving each other, just as in Christ God forgave you."*

Day 4 Through Sacrifice comes Blessing

Look for opportunities to teach your children to forgive. The more they see forgiveness happening at home, the easier it is for them to take that to the outside world and understand what Christ did for them.

Day 5 Your Thoughts and Prayers

_____
_____
_____
_____
_____
_____

WEEK 35

DAY 1

> Do nothing out of selfish ambition or vain conceit, but in humility consider others better than yourselves. Each of you should look not only to your own interests, but also to the interest of others.
>
> Phil. 2:3-4

I'm sure you have heard a saying about "walking a mile in someone else's shoes." I believe this is to remind us that we shouldn't cast judgment on someone's decisions, actions, or thoughts, because we have not been in their circumstances.

After Dan and I married, it seems like the next four years were full of anticipation for his children to move out. I justified my thoughts. After all, his daughter was in her twenties, had two children, and had already been married and divorced. His son had turned 21 and needed to learn life skills and how to function on his own. Well, that happened. Dan's daughter finished college, remarried her first husband, reunited their family, and set out on their own. His son moved into the small house behind us and is learning to take care of himself and a house, while finishing school and working. Awesome!

Strangely, I have now found myself in Dan's shoes. My daughter is about to graduate and get married and my son has only a little bit of high school left. Wait! I'm not ready. My kids still seem so young. They need me. They still have much to learn, and they need to learn at home. Besides, I like having them around. I have always told them, "I not only love you; I like you too." Of course, Dan is looking forward to the "empty nest" syndrome. I thought I was.

I hope you will put yourself in your husband's shoes—especially if he has children from a previous relationship. As much as you love your own children, he loves his just as much. He probably 'likes' having his children around. He probably gets his feelings hurt when you do things or say things to separate your children from his.

I guess I'm writing about this because there is guilt in my heart. I have a new understanding of Dan's feelings. I wish I would have been more understanding, compassionate, and patient. Look at your husband's children while "wearing his shoes". It will hopefully open your eyes and heart to a new love for his precious ones. We have them for only a short time.

> Lord, forgive me for placing barriers between our children, for thinking mine are 'better' and deserve more. Let me see my husband's children through his eyes. Help me see them through Your eyes. Help me love them as my own.

Day 2

Memorize Philippians 2:3-4.

Day 3

You've made it through this devotional book. I am praying that God has spoken to you through it and it has been a good tool for you to use as you mix all the ingredients of your family. I am praying that your family is stronger because of your diligence as a mom. Finally, I am praying that you will be an encouragement to another mom out there who is in our same situation and through sharing your experiences, another mom will become a better "blender".

Day 4 Through Sacrifice comes Blessing

Be in prayer about another mom that you cross paths with that needs to have a word of encouragement from God through you! Just "live out loud" and let God do the rest!

Day 5 Your Thoughts and Prayers

_____
_____
_____
_____
_____
_____

CPSIA information can be obtained at www.ICGtesting.com
Printed in the USA
LVOW13s1004050814

397545LV00020B/247/P